Strategic Acquisition, Divestment, and LBO: Global Dealmaking

Sam P. Dagher, Ph. D.
Professor of Strategic Management and Entrepreneureship
Marywood University

BOOKSURGE PUBLISHING

Copyright © 2007 Dr. Sam P. Dagher
All rights reserved. This publication is protected by Copyright
and permission should be obtained from the author prior to any
prohibited reproduction, storage in a retrieval system, or transmission
in any form or by any means, electronic, mechanical, photocopying,
recording, or likewise.

Published in the United States of America

ISBN: 1-4196-7679-2
ISBN-13: 978-1419676796
Library of Congress Control Number: 2007906670

Visit www.booksurge.com to order additional copies.

*Dedicated to
Glenna, my wife,
My daughter, Lila and her family,
&
My son, Glenn and his family*

Author's Background

Dr. Sam P. Dagher (Samir Phillip) received his Master of Business Administration from Andrews University and his Doctorate (Ph.D.) from Ohio State University. Dr. Dagher has served in various positions in the Bendix Corporation, as Financial Planning Administrator for the Bendix Automotive Aftermarket Operation, Transfer Pricing Coordinator, and Financial Consultant on Acquisition, Divestment, and Operating Problems in the Bendix Corporation at the Executive Offices in Southfield, Michigan.

Dr. Dagher, Professor of Strategic Management and Entrepreneurship at Marywood University in Scranton, Pennsylvania, has served as Executive Director and Chairman of both the graduate and undergraduate business programs at Marywood University and Dean of the School of Business at Aurora University. Sam is a program evaluator for the Association of Collegiate Business Schools and Programs (ACBSP) and serves on the ACBSP Global Business Committee. In addition, he was a member of the Business and Industrial Relations Council of the West Suburban Regional Academic Consortium for Chicago, and a member of the Council for the Illinois Research and Development Corridor. Sam served on various boards of directors, including the Foreign Trade Zone Number 24. He reviewed Title III grants for the U.S. Department of Education and was a member of the Executive Finance Committee as well as a member of the Board of Directors of Marion Hospital. Sam has been a consultant to top management in corporations and higher education and co-presented a series of seminars for the Department of Commerce, Commonwealth of Pennsylvania, entitled "A Guide to Success in Small Business."

Dagher has authored "What Is the Price When a Company Buys From Itself?" published in *Administrative Management* and co-authored "Improving Business Ethics: Poll of Top Managers Stresses, Education, Leadership-by-Example as Strong Forces for Higher Standards," published in the *Management Review*. In addition, he has co-authored "Business Ethics," published in the *Encyclopedia of Management, 3rd ed,* as well as "Global Strategic Acquisitions and Mergers: When the Numbers Are Not Enough," published in the *Conference Proceedings on Globalization and Competition over Trade and Investment Flows*. He has made several presentations at professional conferences that were also published in conference proceedings and has authored a book in two editions entitled, *Corporte Acquisition and Divestment: A Guide to Buying and Selling Business Entities*.

Dr. Dagher's professional memberships include the Academy of Management, the Financial Management Association, and the Association for Corporate Growth.

Preface

In a world of competition and alternative strategies, there are communities that are being structured while others are dismantled due to top management decisions or the economic greed of corporate raiders. Executives use terms such as poison pill, shark repellant, and Pac Man defense, while board members review legal liabilities relative to their fudiciary responsibilities to their shareholders. Could this world have existed prior to mergers, acquisitions, divestments, and leveraged buyouts (LBOs)? Could a person like T. Boone Pickens, who was a geologist from humble beginnings, become a world figure and a threat to Chairmen and CEOs of national and multinational corporations? How did these investment bankers think of introducing the junkbond concept and the covenant lite loan? How did the lawpractice of Henry Kravis end with the dealmaking and leverage buyouts amounting to billions of dollars and dismantling some of the fine corporations of America? Would Kravis be able to perform such a task in China? Where is Chrysler today, which has been acquired by Daimler to form one of the largest automakers of the world, and now ending in the hands of an equity company? Cerberus's acquisition of Chrysler operations and Daimler's divestiture of Chrysler operations combines Europe and the United States with a merger activity and a divestiture one. This particular deal had to be approved by the SEC in the United States (US) and the European Commission (EC) in Europe. The EC under the Maastricht Treaty was able to simply approve the deal because neither customers nor competitors had filed any complaint objecting to this divestiture. The divestiture would no doubt create a major impact on the social and economic life in the Michigan communities since equity companies are known for their interest in immediate return and a quick exit strategy that is concerned with return on investment (ROI) rather than the welfare of society. Where are the legislators? How are corporate lawyers interpreting antitrust laws? Are there any violations? We see democracy and a free enterprise creating a hardship in some of our American communities while some CEOs are receiving unbelievable compensations.

Where are these mergers and acquisitions taking place? They are all over the Western World including the US. They have become part of our daily news. Some are for the good of our communities while others yield more harm than good. Acquisitions, divestments, and LBOs are part of corporate strategic planning and are becoming essential for corporate growth. Although acquisitions have played a great role in corporate strategy in the mid Sixties, it is historically evident that the Seventies have seen the disacquisition approach which the writer refers to as "divestment." Divestment, stated in common terms, is "selling-off" a firm, a division, or a product as an ongoing entity or liquidating the assets. Many scholars use the term "divestiture" and "divestment" interchangeably. In the Eighties and up to the present, corporate America saw a new trend of raiders utilizing its assets as leverage and the term LBO became part of the takeover process.

Structure of the Book

This book describes the theory and practice of strategic acquisitions and divestments. It goes on to explain the structue of LBOs and the role top management plays in the process. Top executives, financial managers, corporate attorneys, junior and senior level finance majors, as well as graduate MBA students should understand the concepts and practical aspects of acquisitions and divestments. The term *organization* is used throughout this text to refer to corporations or business firms that are operating as for-profit organizations; however, the term also applies to not-for-profit organizations that intend to acquire a for-profit company/firm. It is further essential to note that the term *organization* may represent the total corporation as a single entity or a corporation with multi-business operations which may include several firms at the business level that are organized into strategic business units.

Executives at the top, like other individuals, learn from experience how to tackle routine problems. But the most outstanding executive is the one who is able to respond to change. To do this, executives must be on the move in search for knowledge. They must understand the professional terms, strategies, and regulations governing acquisition, divestment, and LBO. Of course, planning and selecting an acquisition or a divestment candidate may lead to the firing or promotion of a top executive. This, in turn, depends on the failure or success of the decision made by the respective executive. If the acquisition and divestment procedure is understood by an executive, then the decision-making process related to this specialized area becomes relatively easy to follow, based on the information requested.

This text covers material related to the decision-making process within national and multi-national organizations. Part I deals with concepts and terms related to the acquisition and divestment process. It introduces the reader, whether executive, financial manager, corporate attorney, or business student, to the various types of acquisitions and divestments. Statutory mergers, statutory consolidation, asset acquisition, stock acquisition, de facto acquisition, tax-free vs. taxable transactions, registered offer vs. tender offer, etc. are presented and a brief summary explaining each term is given. In addition, the writer discusses the changes in The Internal Revenue Code (IRC) which impact "acquisition , divestment, and LBO."

Part II of the text provides useful material for the selection of a business to acquire or the choice of a fully-owned subsidiary to divest. Considerable attention is given to corporate objectives and the financial analysis tools utilized. The role of statutory laws is discussed with considerable emphasis on the relevance of these laws to the Securities and Exchange Commission (SEC) Acts.

Part III focuses on the procedure for acquisitions. The analysis and interpretation of financial statements are covered. Negotiation and investigation of the financial position, as well as the legal liabilities, are discussed. Review of the transaction in line with the SEC regulations and the method of drawing up the final contract, as well as the detailed aspects of the closing process, are included.

Part IV presents divestment vs. retention and the procedure by which a corporation can detect or recognize a divestment candidate. Financial analysis and procedure of the different alternatives that should be used are included. Consideration of SEC requirements are discussed. Key sections of the Internal Revenue Code, as currently amended, are integrated into the procedure, and the tax implications on earnings per share (EPS) are discussed. The complexity of the liquidation vs. the sale of stock with specific points that may develop during the process expose the reader to the practical wealth of knowledge available in parts III and IV of this text.

Part V covers the Leveraged Buyout (LBO) as a process and discussess how it is structured and financed. It further clarifies how the deals are made and what role, if any, does top management play in preventing or facilitating the LBO practice when an outside raider is involved.

Part VI assumes that the reader has read the material presented in Parts I through V and needs a more thorough understanding of its application. Therefore, cases were selected with a complex and comprehensive nature to illustrate the concepts presented. These cases cover decisions related to acquisitions and divestments. Their solutions should be organized and presented in a format that utilizes the procedures outlined in this text.

Acknowledgements

Several people helped to make this book a reality both in a hands-on way and through inspiration. In the Business World, having worked with many executives from various corporations has given me an insight into what this world of corporate acquisitions, divestments, and leveraged buyouts is all about. The deals that were made, and my involvement in making recommendations on certain acquisitions and divestments on the domestic and global scenes have expanded my horizon beyond the borders of the functions of national corporations. In short, several executives, whether directly or indirectly, have contributed to this text through their influence on my thinking. These include, but are not limited to, John Timko, Jr., previously Chairman of the Board of the Foster Wheeler Corporation, William Agee, Previous Chairman and Chief Executive Officer (CEO) of the Bendix Corporation, the architect of the Martin Marietta acquisition, and later Chairman and CEO of Morrisson Knudson Corporation, Dr. W. Michael Blumenthal, Previous Chairman and CEO of the Bendix Corporation, Secretary Treasurer of the US, and later Chairman and CEO of Burroughs Corporation and UNISYS as well as the Designer of the Burroughs and Sperry Univac merger that resulted in UNISYS. Last, but not least, Donald L. Carter, Director of Administration for the Bendix Automotive Operations for his influence in my business career. His encouragement and mentorship role gave me a beginning in business that I will not forget.

Executives, colleagues, professors, and students have enriched this book with their contribution. Special thanks are extended to Gerard R. Roche, Senior Chairman of the Board, Heidrick & Struggles, for agreeing to write the foreword to this book. Gerry has identified top executives throughout the world and placed CEOs in major corporations; some of those that were placed may have been impacted by this topic of acquisitions, divestment, and LBOs. Also, thanks are extended to my colleagues, Dr. Herbert Quigley, Professor of Finance and previous Dean of the School of Business and Government, University of District of Columbia. Herb's comments were very helpful in the formulation of this book. Sincere appreciation to Dr. Henry Amato, Professor of Supply Chain Management and previous Dean of the College of Business Administration, University of Navada, Reno for his observations and remarks that were valuable in putting the content together. My thanks are to Sr. Michele Keenan, I.H.M., Ph.D. previously Vice President of Academic Affairs at Marywood University for her giving me the academic freedom to develop unique and dynamic business programs that stimulated in me the drive to continue my service to others by sharing my knowledge and experience through my teaching and writing of such topics as mergers and divestments. Recognition is inorder to Dr. Steven Kerr, my professor in the doctoral program at Ohio State University for his guidance and influence that instilled in me the goal to design organizational strategies and share my knowledge with others. Dr. Kerr has made extensive contribution to the field of management through his roles as professor, past president of the Academy of Management, and Chief Learning Officer at General Electric and Goldman Sachs. Finally, my thanks are to all my graduate students who have contributed directly and indirectly to this manuscript, especially Nicolas Hanhan for design work and text layout. Furthermore, my gratitude goes to all the staff and publishing consultants of the BookSurge Publishing Company for their effort and contribution in getting this book to its final stage. BookSurge is a wholly owned subsidiary of Amazon.Com and their professional team has been great to work with.

Appreciation is extended to my beloved wife, Glenna Herzog Dagher, for her useful comments and review of this manuscript. My children, Lila Lisa (Dagher) Farley and Glenn William Dagher, have been a continuous inspiration yet practical critics as only offspring can be. Last, but not least, my gratitude goes to Phillip and Lily Dagher, my parents, for creating in me a thirst to pursue the best.

Sam (Samir) Phillip Dagher, Ph.D.

Foreword

The Dow Jones Industrial Average, while rising to a record high this year, has fluctuated around the 14,000 mark. This activity based on the financial news has been fueled by the availability of funds--thus driving up the prices of some of the stocks and causing overvaluation, especially when a list of selected stocks were being acquired at a premium over their current market value. The availability of funds has pushed the worldwide mergers and acquisition market up to approximately 2.7 trillion dollars, according to the Association for Corporate Growth's survey and Thomson Financial. These types of funds are slowly evaporating--thus reducing the takeover activities and bringing this financial sector into volatile and serious jeopardy.

Dr. Sam Dagher in this book deals with how these topics are handled and presents a guide to the merger, acquisition, and divestment that top management can use in the design of their corporate grand strategy. Sam further explains the various types of acquisitions and divestments and how these acquisitions and divestments are successfully accomplished. He discusses the leveraged buyout (LBO) structure dealing with LBO activities across borders and detailing the complexities that can arise in the global arenas. In addition, he points out how to acquire and why to acquire, along with what to acquire focusing on the acquisition process and discussing the negotiation as well as the investigation procedure surrounding the target company's financial position and the legal liabilities associated with the acquisition process. He presents the concept of divestment and covers the procedure by which a corporation can identify or recognize a candidate for divestment. Sam explains the SEC requirement covering sections of the 1933 and 1934 Acts related to both acquisitions and divestment. He clearly highlights the role of the European Commission in the acquisition and divestment process and relates that to the SEC role in the US, pointing out what sections cover cross borders' regulations that a divestor or an acquirer must consider prior to attempting a cross border transaction in this field.

In my judgment, this book serves as a comprehensive guide to acquiring, divesting, and structuring LBO transactions. It should be of great interest to members of the Association for Corporate Growth as well as to Senior Undergraduate and MBA students, investment bankers, board members, and chief executive officers who are trying to learn more about this field. Furthermore, chief financial officers and controllers should be aware of the method of financing an acquisition and how to evaluate reinvestment opportunities. Their approach to reinvesting the proceeds from a divestment or the evaluation of whether to finance an acquisition through debt or equity or a combination of both are easily answered in this particular text. It is essential to note that the way in which Dr. Dagher presents the subject matter and the method through which he illustrates the analytical process of potential candidates would benefit any serious reader of this book.

Gerard R. Roche
Senior Chairman
Heidrick & Struggles

TABLE OF CONTENTS

LIST OF TABLES — xiii

PART ONE
TYPES OF ACQUISITIONS AND DIVESTMENTS

Chapter
1. STRATEGIC ACQUISITIONS AND DIVESTMENTS — 3
2. TAX IMPLICATIONS — 11
3. SECURITIES EXCHANGE ROLE — 15

PART TWO
PLANNING AND SELECTING AN ACQUISITION OR A DIVESTMENT

4. BUSINESS KNOWLEDGE AND BUYERS' OBJECTIVES — 21
5. FINANCIAL DATA AND ANALYSIS OF ACQUISITION CANDIDATES — 27
6. DIVESTMENT EVALUATION AND THE FIRM'S PLAN — 35
7. RELATED STATUTORY LAWS VS. SECURITIES AND EXCHANGE LAWS — 43

PART THREE
ACQUISITION PROCEDURE

8. CANDIDATE IDENTIFICATION AND PURCHASE DETERMINATION — 53
9. NEGOTIATION AND INVESTIGATION OF ACCOUNTING AND LEGAL RECORDS — 67
10. ACQUISITION CONSIDERATIONS OF OVERSEAS COMPANIES — 75
11. ACQUISITION CONTRACT AND THE CLOSING PROCESS — 79

PART FOUR
DIVESTMENT PROCEDURE

12. DIVESTMENT VS. RETENTION: CANDIDATE RECOGNITION — 87
13. FINANCIAL COMPARISON OF RETENTION, DIVESTMENT, AND REINVESTMENT ALTERNATIVES — 95
14. TAX IMPLICATIONS AND CONSIDERATIONS IN DOMESTIC AND INTERNATIONAL DIVESTMENTS — 103
15. SALE OF STOCK VS. LIQUIDATION: THE CLOSING PROCESS — 107

PART FIVE
LEVERAGED BUY OUT (LBO)

16	THE LBO CONCEPT	125
17	LBO ACTIVITIES AND COMPLEXITIES	131

PART SIX CASES

1	MANUFACTURER'S CORPORATION DIVESTMENT OF THE ELECTRODYNAMICS COMPANY (HYPOTHETICAL CASE STUDY)	139
2	CHEVRON'S ACQUISITION OF UNOCAL CORPORATION (ACQUISITION CASE STUDY)	145

APPENDICES

A	INTERNAL REVENUE CODE SECTIONS 331, 332, 333, 334, 337, 341, 362, 368	151
B	SEC SCHEDULE 14D-1, AND SCHEDULE 13G WITH INSTRUCTIONS	167
C	SEC SCHEDULE 13D WITH INSTRUCTIONS ALONG WITH PAGE 3 THROUGH PAGE 5 OF THE BENDIX SEC SUBMISSION	178

GLOSSARY	186

INDEX	195

TABLES

8.1	Estimated Value of "J" Equity	59
8.2	Estimated Value of "J" Investment	60
8.3	J's 51% Estimated Equity Value	61
8.4	Corporation J Consolidated Balance Sheet	62
8.5	"M" Additional Profits	64
12.1	Divestment Ranking Analysis	92
15.1	Summary of Actual Sales and Profits For S & D	110
15.2	S & D Balance Sheet	111
15.3	S & D Summary of Projected Sales and Profit	112
15.4	S & D Stock Sale Alternative	113
15.5	S & D Non-Recurring Closing Costs	115
15.6	S & D Assumptions Used in Calculating the Liquidation Alternative Percent of Recovery	116
15.7	S & D Asset Recovery Values	117
15.8	S & D Cash Proceeds and Investment Liquidation	118
15.9	S & D Tax Benefits From Liquidation	119
15.10	S & D Cash Flow From Liquidation	120
15.11	S & D Impact of Liquidation on XYZ Corporation	121

PART ONE

Types of Acquisitions and Divestments

CHAPTER 1

STRATEGIC ACQUISITIONS AND DIVESTMENTS

Are acquisitons and divestments a part of the corporate grand strategies?

What are the two types of acquisitions?

What are the three ways in which an acquisition may be carried out?

What are some of the reasons for an acquisition?

What are the differences among vertical, horizontal, and conglomerate growth?

Why else might a company be acquired?

What is "divestment"?

What are the four types of divestment?

What are some of the reasons for divestment?

Strategic Acquisitions And Divestments

Corporate mergers and divestments are an essential part of major corporate grand strategies. They represent management's intention to maximize shareholders' wealth. This intention is geared to select a strategic approach for growth. Thus growth becomes a part of a corporate grand strategy. This grand strategy may include different types of acquisitons or divestments and may lead a company either to horizontal integration or vertical integration, or in some cases to diversification, thus having the ultimate goal of maximizing wealth to the shareholders.

Therefore, an executive may wonder how Company X selected and acquired Company Y. What was available to Company X, and what options did Company X have? These complex questions are derived from factors that may have contributed to the success of Company X. To what is this success attached? No doubt, it is related to the Chief Executive Officer's (CEO's) intention which in turn is connected to the company's grand strategy.

The CEO along with top management establish a long-term direction for the organization. This long-term direction sets the managerial decisions and action steps that determine the organization's performance in the long-run. These action steps are developed in the pursuit of organizational goals and are supported by specific objectives which are then linked to strategies that focus on achieving these structured goals. Thus such a process helps the CEO relate to turbulent and complex situations that may result in a divestment or a strategic merger. These unforseen situations are projected and planned for through a proactive strategy, but this strategy may have to change into an aggressive reactive one, depending on the projected environmental conditions or the unforseen environmental situations that may arise. Therefore, the CEO's strategic approach may be designed to select a grand strategy that is based on the environmental analysis done which takes into consideration the internal environment of strengths and weaknesses of the organization as well as the external environment of the opportunities that may exist or are projected to exist along with the threats that the competition may be exercising or planning to exercise. These environmental factors along with others can lead to the success or failure of a merger. Thus success leads executives to ask the question, "How can WE do it?". Previous to describing the complicated process of acquisition, an executive must comprehend certain basic terms which are explained in subsequent paragraphs.

STRATEGIC MERGERS/CORPORATE GRAND STRATEGIES

It is important to recognize that a firm/organization should know the direction it wants to follow. The CEO can set a visionary approach by working with the Board of Directors of his/her organization to establish this direction. In doing so, the CEO is structuring a plan which in common business terms may be called a strategic plan. This strategic plan will then identify the mission of the organization along with the goals and objectives that are in support of the mission. A clear mission statement for the organization should be formulated after a complete, thorough analysis of the organization's/firm's external and internal environments. Analysis of the firm's environments will help identify the firm's options and select the best strategic alternative to which a set of long-term goals and grand strategies can be developed. These long-term goals and grand strategies will provide the organization/firm with the direction for strategic actions. Some of these grand strategies may include the following:

- Concentric growth
- Market/product development
- Horizontal integration
- Vertical integration
- Concentric diversification
- Conglomerate diversification
- Joint ventures/strategic alliances
- Divestments
- Bankruptcy/reorganization
- Liquidation

INTERPRETATION OF GRAND STRATEGIES

Grand strategies are the ones that provide the corporate direction. As noted earlier, they are the strategic actions that lead toward achieving the long term objectives of the firm. Some authors may include innovation as a grand strategy, but for the sake of this discussion the aforementioned ten grand strategies will be discussed since they encompass some of the grand strategies that others may include seperately such as turnaround strategy, innovation, etc.

The concentric growth strategy which is listed as part of strategic mergers may lead a company to emphasize a single product in a single market with a single dominant technology to pursue horizontal acquisitions if the concentrated growth would yield stable market conditions and favorable competitive advantage. However, such a pursuit may be vulnerable to changing environmental factors that may impact the firm negatively. The risk in pursuing such a strategy is further discussed in other chapters of this text. Relative to market/product development strategies, the approach differs in that market development consists of marketing the current product, with minor modification, to other customers in related markets through different channels of distribution or through a modification of the current advertising strategy or by invading other geographic areas while product development, on the other hand, deals with major modification of current products for new applications or the development of related products to be marketed to the current customers. The horizontal integration is another grand strategy that is based on the acquisition of similar firms while the vertical integration approach depends mainly on the acquisition of suppliers or distributors or both of them, depending on whether the firm is using a backward or a forward integration strategy or a combination of the two. In the concentric diversification strategy, the firm pursues the approach that would minimize loss and maximize its stock value: thus a spin-off strategy may be used in establishing a separate business entity with synergy supporting its own product but not negatively impacting its profitability. An example of concentric diversification would be the Pepsi Corporation spin-off of KFC, Pizza Hut, and Taco Bell into a separate entity which later acquired AW and Long John Silver and is currently operating under the Yum name. While concentric diversification emphasizes market synergy, conglomorate diversification expands in various business markets seeking maximization of return and minimization of risk by diversifying into unrelated industries.

Firms seeking expansions sometimes do not seek to acquire but rather partner with other firms, thus joining financial and technological as well as managerial resourses. The fact that financial resources are involved give the participating firms equity positions, thus leading them into what is called a joint venture. However, if the firms' partnerships exist for a limited period of time and the contribution that each partner is making is limited to technology, professional, and managerial skills, but excludes investments and equity ownership, then such a venture is referred to as a strategic alliance. In some cases, a company may review its operation and may find that a division or a subsidiary is not aligned with its corporate goals. If this is the case, a decision to sell the operation outright or spin-off the assets may be made in order to enhance corporate profitability or achieve corporate goals. Such an action step may be referred to as a divestment. The topics of divestments, and the sub-topics of reorganization, bankruptcy, and liquidation are discussed thoroughly in other chapters of this book following the explanation of the acquisition and strategic merger terms.

TYPES OF ACQUISITIONS/STRATEGIC MERGERS

There are two commonly known types of acquisitions: (1) the traditional acquisition is one in which an agreement is negotiated and drawn between a willing seller and a willing buyer, and (2) the take-over acquisition is one in which the buyer makes a direct bid to the seller's stockholders despite the opposition of the seller's management. To help clarify the distinction between the traditional acquisition and the takeover, it may be helpful to remember that the first is done with full management approval and participation while the latter is completed with negative interaction on the part of the seller's management. However, in the case of a takeover, the buyer is acquiring the outstanding stock of the seller without the seller's management consent. This type of acquisition is strictly a stock acquisition. Stock acquisition, therefore, may be traditional or take-over, depending on the manner in which it is accomplished.

There are sub-classifications of the traditional type of acquisition that must be clearly understood. These may involve (1) merger/strategic merger, (2) asset acquisition, or (3) consolidation. A merger is a combination of two or more companies into one. However, this merger can be a strategic merger if it focuses on delivering customer value, increased revenue/profit, or a product differentitation approach which otherwise cannot be achieved without such a merger. A good example of a strategic merger is the acquisition of Compaq Computer Corporation by Hewlett-Packard. A single entity is then in existence carrying the name of one of the merged companies. A merger can be called either statutory or de facto. A statutory merger centers on the combination of two or more firms/companies pursuant to the requirement of the law of the state of incorporation while in a de facto merger, the buyer acquires all of the seller's assets by involving the buyer's securities and without a formal notice to the seller's stockholders.

Although the term "merger" is most commonly used, the asset acquisition and the consolidation may be exercised in an acquisition process. The asset acquisition takes into consideration the process in which the buyer acquires all or part of the seller's assets, while the consolidation involves the combination of two or more firms, thus forming a completely new corporation. This new corporation absorbs all the consolidated companies with a new name. A good example of a consolidation is DaimlerChrysler Corporation.

WHY ACQUIRE?

Expansion and return on investment (ROI) can be reasons/strategies for acquisitions. However, acquisition of an on-going concern is just as complicated as internal expansion. What remains as the basic reason/strategy for an acquisition can be part of the underlying process in the buyer's objectives for the acquisition. These objectives may include, but are not limited to, the following: (1) need for a new product, (2) need for additional space, (3) need for holding a certain patent, (4) need for technical expertise in product development and/or management talent, (5) need for increased market share and/or increased sales, and (6) need for independence from suppliers. The achievement of these objectives can be the answer to the intended acquisition.

If the intended acquisition is for corporate growth, it can be either classified as vertical, horizontal, or conglomerate. Thus, the grand strategies of the corporation provide the basic direction. These grand strategies become the core business strategies of the firm. Therefore, the "why acquire?" concept will depend on the intention of the CEO which is derived from the corporate strategic plan. If the acquisition is for independence from certain suppliers or distributors, then the buyer's company may seek to acquire one of its suppliers or one of its distributors, thus eliminating the dependency on either the supplier or the distributor, then such an acquisition is intended for vertical growth/integration. However, if the buyer's company chooses to acquire one of its competitors, then such an acquisition is for horizontal growth/integration. Nevertheless, if the buyer's company selects an acquisition candidate that is neither a supplier, distributor, nor a competitor but is strictly in an unrelated line of business, then the acquisition is intended for conglomerate growth/diversification. Therefore, the buyer's intention is part of the corporate strategy which in some cases may be for concentrated growth which may require the direction of a firm's resources towards the product lines that are most profitable. In such a situation, a company may be after the market share of a certain product line and thus may be interested in growing by building on its competencies and concentrating on the product or market segment in which it has the best know-how.

"Why acquire?" can be neither for conglomerate growth nor for horizontal expansion, but for the sole purpose of acquiring management talent. This is usually done when other attempts at obtaining the competitor's managerial personnel have failed. However, caution must be exercised in this case. Evaluation of all risks associated with such an acquisition's objective must be done and the consequences of the results of such a "marriage" should be carefully weighed.

However, the motives of companies towards acquisition has taken a new direction lately. This new direction has involved a primary approach to labor outsourcing which has exported jobs overseas through the acquisition of wholly owned subsidiaries and through the structure of joint ventures. These areas will be discussed in detail later in this book because job outsourcing has become one of the multinational corporate strategies for cost reduction. Another motive for acquiring a company may be for tax consideration. Tax considerations are, therefore, essential in the evaluation of the acquisition. These considerations involve the pre-planning of a "tax-free" acquisition which revolves around tax-postponement rather than around a taxable event. (Further implications of tax consequences are discussed in Chapter 2.)

DIVESTMENT--DEFINITION AND TYPES

Divestment is the process of eliminating a portion of a line of business or the firm as a whole and using the freed resources for some other purpose. A question that is often raised by businessmen is, "What is the difference between a divestment and a liquidation?" Liquidation is, in fact, a type of divestment. If there is no hope for a continued profitable operation of a firm, then liquidation is the only remaining alternative solution.

If liquidation is a type, what other types of divestment exist? Divestment, in fact, has recently been acknowledged as an important strategy in corporate long-range planning. It has been the diagnostic treatment of symptoms of expected corporate failures. Types of divestment include (1) sale of stock, (2) sale of a product line, (3) sale of a whole division, and (4) liquidation of a product, division, or subsidiary.

WHY DIVEST?

The effects of divestment are more far-reaching than what is generally publicized. Although top management is usually actively involved in divestment, divisional management rarely knows what to expect until after a negotiated agreement between the buyer and seller is drawn.

Reasons for divestment can include, but are not limited to, the following: (1) corporate objectives of improved profits and higher ROI, (2) corporate cash needs, (3) better investment opportunities in a different line of business, (4) change in top management or a change in corporate strategy, and (5) government rules and regulations, such as the Federal Trade Commission (FTC) ruling forcing conglomerates to divest certain operations.

The "why divest?" concept is becoming an essential aspect of corporate success or failure. The investment opportunities available elsewhere are attracting executives to identify "sick" products and "weak" divisions for divestment in order to utilize the funds for reinvestment. This procedure is becoming a treatment to the deteriorating profits which, in turn, may be an answer to the "why divest?" phrase. (Detailed explanations are covered in Chapters 6, 12, and 13.)

CHAPTER 2

TAX IMPLICATIONS

What are the acquirer's tax goals?

What are the divestor's tax goals?

What are the steps in determining whether a transaction should be taxable or tax-free?

Acquisitions and divestments can be accomplished either through a cash or stock transaction, depending on the approaches selected by management of the "divestor" (seller) or the "acquirer" (buyer). A popular question that is often raised by corporate executives is: Will the transaction be taxable or tax-free? Surely, this complex question is based upon the fact that taxation of "acquisitions and divestments" is classified into categories as outlined by specific sections of the Internal Revenue Code (IRC). For example, Section 368 of the IRC refers to corporate reorganization. The term reorganization is interpreted to mean a statutory merger or consolidation which is further explained as the "acquisition by one corporation, in exchange solely for all or a part of its voting stock ...."[1]

Further details regarding the most common types of reorganization are shown in Section 368, paragraphs (a) (1) (A), (B), (C) and (D).[2] However, the type of payment which the stockholders receive can determine the taxability of the transaction. But what remain to be defined are the goals and specific objectives of the acquirer vis-a-vis that of the divestor.

The 1986 Tax Reform Act (TRA) has repealed certain provisions of Sections 333, 336, and 337 of the IRC. However, favorable treatment for capital gains was also repealed, thus impacting parts of Section 331 which provided that amounts received by shareholders as part of a complete liquidation are treated as payment for shareholder's stock. Therefore, the effects of a liquidation on shareholders' gain or loss may be impacted.

Section 333 was repealed and therefore impacts the postponement for the recognition of gain by a shareholder upon receipt of funds in a liquidating distribution.

Section 337 has been completely revised to provide "nonrecognition for property distributed to parent in complete liquidation of subsidiary." This nonrecognition regulation applies to those distributions in satisfaction for treatment of indebtedness by a subsidiary to a parent company as well as to distributions in exchange for stock. However, Section 337, paragraphs (a) through (c) were repealed and replaced by Section 631, paragraph (a) of Public Law 99-514.

These original Sections 331, 333, 336, and 337 of the IRC along with the amendments affecting them are shown in Appendix A.

ACQUIRER'S TAX GOALS

The purchase price is the determining factor in the type of transaction that the acquirer should pursue during the negotiation process.

---

1 This particular section is shown in Appendix A of this book.
2 Ibid.

Usually, the acquirer requests a taxable transaction if the purchase price is in excess of the divestor's tax cost. For example, if the divestor's total business has a taxable value of $100,000 and the acquirer is willing to acquire it for $200,000, the difference of the $100,000 will be considered as goodwill. The acquirer, in such a case, should insist on a taxable transaction that will allow the write-up of non-current assets. This write-up would increase the acquirer's depreciation —thus impacting the pre-tax profit depending on the depreciation method used. Previous to the amendment of the laws relative to goodwill, this approach would have been the best route for an acquirer to follow. However, since goodwill can now be amortized over a fifteen year period, and will impact the corporate pre-tax profit, the alternative of writing up the fixed asset would, under the current laws, defer taxes into a future period.

The goal for the acquirer in the previously stated example must be to increase the value of the assets acquired and defer the tax liability. However, this type of an approach must give careful consideration to future intended divestment which should be based on the IRC Sections 332, 351, and 362. A detailed explation of these sections and others are shown in Appendix A; however, Chapter 14 elaborates further on the important sections related to divestment.

DIVESTOR'S TAX GOALS

The basic tax goals of a divestor always take into consideration the purchase price offered by the acquirer. Generally, the divestor and the acquirer are interested in tax deferral as well as tax minimization.

The tax free reorganization as described in Section 358 of the IRC results in no gain or loss to the security holders of the acquirer or the divestor if the transaction structured is a stock exchange.

The tax impact to the acquirer is as important as it is to the divestor. The divestor might dictate the method of acquisition by the divestment method implemented. The divestor may decide on a liquidation transaction rather than the sale of an on-going business. This is usually determined after a calculation is done of the tax implications. If the divestor would have chosen to proceed with a liquidation plan under section 337, Paragraph (a), then the gain or loss from the divestment would have been impacted by the content of this cited paragraph which states that "if, within the 12 month period beginning on the date on which a corporation adopts a plan of complete liquidation, all the assets of the corporation are distributed in the liquidation, less assets retained to meet claims, then no gain or loss shall be recognized to such disposition…"[3]

---

3   Ibid, Appendix A: Sec. 337 has been repealed.

This method of divestment can assist both the acquirer and the divestor in obtaining the Internal Revenue Service (IRS) approval for a partial tax-free transaction. However, procedural steps must be carefully outlined and followed in order to avoid any deviation from the interpretation of the revised section 337. This plan can and should be structured in light of Sections 1245 and 1250 of the IRC, which describes the gain from disposition of depreciable assets.

How to Determine Whether the Transaction Should be Taxable or Tax-Free?

To determine the type of transaction that should be chosen, answers to the following questions should be sought:

1. Is the asset or the stock being acquired?
2. What type of payment is the acquirer planning to make?
3. Is the payment going to be in stock or in cash?
4. Is the transaction a statutory merger (i.e.) does it meet state laws?

If the asset or stock is acquired, and the payment is in stock or shares, while the acquisition meets statutory laws, then the transaction qualifies as a reorganization which can be either a statutory merger or a consolidation, depending on whether one of the companies absorbs the other or both companies vanish and a new entity composed of the two emerges. This type of reorganization qualifies as a tax-free transaction.

However, compliance with the state law may create problems. These problems involve meeting the demands of shareholders of the divested company. To avoid such problems, the use of a subsidiary as the acquiring company can be implemented.

Careful consideration must be taken by the tax planners if the answer to question three(3) is stocks and bonds. To qualify the transaction for a tax-free treatment, the majority of the payment must be in stock, otherwise the reorganization will be treated as a taxable transaction.

FURTHER IMPLICATIONS

The various Sections of the IRC specified in this chapter are not the only factors that the divestor and the acquirer must review. Basic problem areas which may affect the substance of the transaction must be reviewed. These areas involve the Federal Securities Laws. These laws impact the public, the divestors, creditors, and the stockholders of both the acquiring company and the one being acquired. A discussion of these laws and the role the Security Exchange Commission (SEC) plays in enforcing them follows in Chapter 3.

CHAPTER 3

SECURITIES EXCHANGE ROLE

What federal government agencies must be informed about a potential acquisition attempt?

What types of acquisitions are exempt from notification?

Whom does each federal government agency try to protect?

The Securities and Exchange Commission (SEC) is a government agency established in 1934 and charged with the responsibilities of (1) requiring public disclosure of pertinent facts, (2) enforcing disclosure requirements in the soliciting of monies, (3) regulating the trading in securities on national security exchanges, (4) investigating securities fraud and enforcing legal sanctions against such violations, (5) requiring the registration of securities brokers dealers and investment, (6) administering statutory standards, (7) regulating the purchase and sale of securities, and (8) advising federal courts in corporate reorganization.[1]

THE 1933 AND 1934 SEC ACTS

To perform the above functions, the SEC enforces the Securities Acts passed by Congress. For example, the Securities Act of 1933 requires any offering of securities for sale to file information with the Federal Trade Commission (FTC) on the financial condition of the issuing corporation.[2]

The 1934 SEC Act initially created the SEC agency and transferred the functions and responsibility from the FTC to the SEC agency. In addition, the 1934 SEC Act requires corporations whose securities are traded to file financial reports with the SEC agency.[3]

The SEC agency has a special corporate financial division as part of the commission structure. This division mainly establishes standards for financial reports and examines and monitors corporate activities. Therefore, any activity by a corporation to acquire control of another corporation must be reported to the SEC. The requirement applies to all corporations whose securities are traded on the national exchange. However, for further information regarding the SEC activities, material can be obtained online from the website, www.sec.gov/.

SEC VS. FTC

The SEC is not the only government agency that requires notification in any acquisition process. The FTC also requires pre-acquisition notification. This is based on Section Seven of the Clayton Act. A major concern of the FTC is that an acquisition may create unfair competition which would impact the public at large. The requirement for filing with the SEC, therefore, becomes a must.

Certain waiting periods can be realized if an acquisition meets stated criteria. One of these stated criteria is the share the acquiring company will hold of the voting securities or assets

---

1   "Securities and Exchange Commission," *Congressional Quarterly's, Inc., Federal Regulatory Directory*, Washington, D.C. 20037.
2   Ratner, David L. and Thomas Lee Hazen. Eds. *Securities Regulation in a Nutshell*. (St. Paul: Thomson West, 2005), 38-100.
3   Ibid. 101-184.

of the divested company. Careful review by the legal counsel of Section 802.20 Par. (6) of the FTC rules must be done prior to any acquisition process.

Exemption from filing notification with the FTC can be realized if the acquisition and divestment lies within certain guidelines. Some of these guidelines include but are not limited to the following:

> (1) The acquisition of non-voting securities, (i.e.) bonds, mortgages, deeds, etc.
>
> (2) The acquirer owns 50% or more of the divestor voting stock prior to such acquisition process.
>
> (3) The acquisition attempt will not create an ownership of five percent (5%) or more of a company's equity securities by the acquirer.

A sample of the notification form with an explanation of the information needed is presented in Chapter Seven and Appendices B and C.

RESPONSIBILITY AND METHOD OF FILING

The SEC and the FTC notification requirement must be discussed by the divestor and the acquirer at the initiation of the negotiation process and prior to the signing of any formal agreement. However, in a negotiation transaction where the divestor and the acquirer representatives are trying to arrive at an agreeable contract, both parties must file notification with the FTC. With regard to SEC, the notification must be filed only if the corporations are listed on the national exchange or are sold over the counter where public interest is impacted. The SEC in this case is trying to protect the investor while the FTC is trying to protect the end consumer.

Filing of notification is required by the SEC of the acquirer only if the acquisition process is a tender-offer or a take-over bid. The SEC requires the acquirer to file a 13-D within 10 days of the acquisition event or as soon as the acquirer has completed purchasing 5% or more of equity in any company it intends to acquire. However, the FTC requires both the acquirer and the target company to file a notification. This is clearly stated in Section 801.30 of the FTC Rules. These Rules state that the target corporation must file on the 19th day after the date of the receipt by the acquirer. If the transaction is a cash tender offer, the target date becomes the 10th day. Therefore, it is very essential for the acquirer to review Section 801.3 along with Sections 801.2 and 801.4 of the FTC. It is recommended that this review be done on-line by going to **www.ftc.gov/** since these rules are regularly reviewed and amended and an interpretation of changing the policy is provided for all concerned.

SEC REGISTRATION REQUIREMENTS

Section 5 of the SEC 1933 Act states that unless a registration statement is in effect with the SEC, it is unlawful for any corporation or individual to offer to sell, or to sell, such security to the public. Under this section of the Act, it is essential that a clear statement of the nature of the transaction be filed with the SEC. If the acquirer utilizes its stock to acquire a divested company, whether the stock is treasury or newly issued, it is important to note that the transaction requires then a revision of the registration statement and consequent filing with the SEC within the allotted time period.

The divestor is also responsible for filing a revised registration statement under Section 2 of the 1933 Act. However, exemptions can exist for either the acquirer or the divestor if they are non-public and privately held companies. This type of exemption is discussed in section 4 of the 1933 SEC Act.

Guidelines regarding the exemption are provided by the SEC. These guidelines include, but are not limited to (1) the number of the acquirer's stockholders, (2) the number of shares issued, (3) the nature of the investment, and (4) the financial data available to the potential stockholders.

Complexity of Law and Commission Interpretations

Outside legal consultants' advice is always a good approach for both the acquirer and the divestor. Interpretation of the various sections within the SEC Acts that might impact the transaction is a must.

Communication at earlier stages with the SEC regarding registration and filing requirements is advisable. If the SEC believes that the acquirer or divestor is exempt from filing a registration statement, a request by the exempt party, for written confirmation from the SEC must be obtained. However, careful consideration and review of the statutory laws by the acquirer and the divestor must be done. These state laws can sometimes hinder an acquisition or a divestment if the transaction was not structured in line with corporate state laws.

Further discussion regarding this topic is covered in Chapter 7.

PART TWO

Planning and Selecting an Acquisition or a Divestment

CHAPTER 4

BUSINESS KNOWLEDGE AND BUYER'S OBJECTIVES

What types of information are needed to analyze the market for a proposed acquisition?

What are some of the trade-offs to be considered before an acquisition is attempted?

What are some of the factors that an acquiring company should review in its own performance?

What does the buyer's long-range plan include?

What specific elements must the plan include?

What screening criteria should a buyer use?

Acquisition of an on-going business, as stated in earlier chapters, may be an accelerated means of achieving growth. However, the choice of a firm to be acquired is not an easy task. The buyer should know the line of business and the prospect in detail. The buyer should focus on long-term rather than short-term objectives. Short-term profitability through the combination of business entities may have a negative long-term impact on the buyer's own business.

The information obtained by the buyer and the process by which the buyer approaches an acquisition should be part of the objectives. Evaluation of the candidate's manufacturing plant, personnel, and cash and sales capabilities must be done by the buyer. In other words, the buyer should determine the capabilities and drawbacks of the acquisition candidate.

Acquisition procedures such as that of Hewlett-Packard (HP) in its acquisition of Compaq Computer Corporation is not a mere accident but a designed strategy. This strategy involved careful analysis and evaluation of the goals and objectives of HP as well as the analysis of Compaq Computer operations. Evaluation of an acquisition candidate such as Compaq should not be the sole task of the CEO such as Carly Fiorina's of HP but should include the market expansion and stability over the next five years of the acquiring company. In the case of HP, the acquisition of Compaq would have encompassed elements from the strategic plan which would include the following:

1. Present and future product lines of the buyer's organization.

2. Present and future product lines of the business to be acquired.

3. Past and future performance of the candidate to be acquired, including product prices, costs, and industry trends.

4. Capital expenditure required by the acquirer/buyer to make the business efficient

5. Type of management and technical personnel needed for such an operation.

6. Past and future financial status of the candidate under evaluation. This financial information should include income statement, a balance sheet, break-even analysis, return on assets (ROA) analysis, and statement of sources and uses of funds.

All the preceding information must be coupled with a thorough analysis of the market and a relative comparison to the information obtained.

MARKET ANALYSIS

The acquirer's objectives are essential in determining the purpose of the market analysis. These objectives should provide the acquirer with the basis for corrective actions and control which lead to the review of the total market potential for the product lines identified. The total market potential is essential. However, the market share of the firm being acquired is as important as the total market potential.

The acquirer's marketing strategy should be outlined prior to any acquisition attempt. This marketing strategy should identify basic strategic trade-offs facing the buyer's organization. These trade-offs would include some of the following basic factors:

1. Short-term gain versus long-term growth.

2. Growth versus continued financial stability.

3. Profit margins versus market competition.

4. Risk-free investment versus high and low risk acquisitions.

The question remains: What are the objectives of the acquirer? For example, was the acquisition of Autolite by the Bendix Corporation done in line with Bendix's corporate long-range plans? The Bendix corporate objectives were surely outlined prior to the attempt of such an acquisition. The marketing strategy in the automotive area was a grand design for achieving corporate objectives. The segmentation of the market to serve both original equipment manufacturers (OEM) as well as the after market operation (AMO) made the acquisition necessary.

Buyer's objectives may be not only for segmentation by product line/channel of distribution, but also geographical. Geographical segmentation of the corporation would take into consideration the weakness of the competition and the market potential available, as well as the market share. For example, The Bendix Corporation acquisition of Societe Anonyme de Bendix (DBA), which is currently a Bendix Corporation subsidiary, was not only for improvement of earnings per share (EPS). Although EPS was one of the corporate objectives, another long-range objective was the corporation's international marketing strategy which involved geographical segmentation and improvement of its international market share in the automotive, as well as aerospace, lines of business.

So in a thorough review of an acquisition candidate, the acquirer must carefully review its own company's performance as well as that of the candidate's performance. This review should address itself to the following factors:

1. The future pricing strategy of the firm's products, e.g. is the firm using the right pricing method (cost plus mark-up or competitive) and should such a method continue to be utilized?

2. Future direct and indirect labor cost (i.e.) what type of a union contract is the buyer acquiring?

3. The market strategy of the acquirer as well as that of the candidate being acquired. This should be reviewed in line with the existing and expected competition.

4. The trends within the industry.

5. The technological changes that might impact the future level of production.

LONG-RANGE PLAN

Much of what has been discussed in this chapter is a part of long-range planning. The development of the long-range plan for a buyer should include: (a) list of objectives, (b) specific targets, (c) budgets, and (d) tactics for accomplishing these objectives. The plan, in fact, must have four important elements. These elements are as follows: (1) Which industries show future growth? (2) How do these industries complement the buyer's business? (3) How do the manufacturing techniques of these industries vary from the buyer's business? and (4) How are these manufacturing techniques similar to the buyer's business?

As stated earlier, if the objective of the buyer is to grow through diversification, thus eliminating the risk of financial instability, then the approach is termed unsystematic, and the concern is mainly acquisition for stabilization or improvement of EPS. However, if the buyer's objective is growth and market penetration in addition to market segmentation, then the approach is termed systematic in that the risk of lower future EPS may exist. But whatever the approach might be, a buyer's screening criteria in the acquisition process should define what the buyer requires in terms of the following:

1. The size of the business should be considered since the acquisition process is the same for a small or large business.

2. The return on investment should be carefully analyzed.

3. The potential growth in sales for the acquired candidate should be projected.

4. The management personnel requirement should be estimated.

5. The sales distribution, as well as the market share, should be analyzed.

6. The competitor's performance must be carefully scrutinized by reviewing the candidate's five year revenues, profit margin, pre-tax profit, net assets employed, and the ROA and ROI.

All these elements must be considered in line with additional promotional programs, updated technology, current management weaknesses, and future managerial strength. But regardless of what the outcome of this analysis is, the concern of the buyer could focus on a non-taxable acquisition transaction for cash flow purposes. The impact on taxes on the acquisition process is not the only concern that the buyer might have. The financial analysis of the data for the acquisition candidate and the study of the accounting method to be used for the acquisition should be of great concern to the buyer. These concerns and the different approaches for handling them are the subject of the next chapter.

CHAPTER 5

FINANCIAL DATA AND ANALYSIS OF ACQUISITION CANDIDATES

What standard sources of financial information are available for use in a preliminary evaluation of a publicly held company?

What non-financial information should also be collected in a preliminary evaluation of a company?

What are the three ways of analyzing the price that a buyer should consider in determing the value of an acquisition candidate?

What are the two basic accounting methods for handling an acquisition?

What financial reports should be reviewed?

The financial data of a prospect or acquisition candidate is as important in the preliminary decision process as it is in the final decision. Evaluation of the financial data is paramount in managerial decision processes, as well as in meeting the SEC disclosure regulations. In addition, such data are required by the Internal Revenue Service (IRS), as well as the buyer's external auditors if the buyer is a publicly owned company.

Once the acquisition candidate is selected, the financial data required for preliminary analysis can be obtained from external sources. A considerable amount of information for this review could come from either or all of the following sources:

1. *Moody's Industrial Reports*
2. *Value Line Reports*
3. *Dun and Bradstreet Reports*
4. *Standard and Poor's Reports*
5. *Robert Morris Association Reports*
6. *Barron's Guide*
7. Annual & Quarterly Stockholders Reports of the corporation being acquired
8. Proxy Statements
9. *Securities Exchange Commission Reports* - (i.e.) 10-K, 10-Q, etc. available on line at www.sec.gov/
10. Professional publications such as *The Wall Street Journal, Business Week, Forbes, Fortune 500, Financial World,* Financial Times, etc.

These listed sources would be helpful if the acquisition candidate is a publicly owned firm. However, if the firm selected for acquisition is a closely held company, (i.e.) a subchapter S family corporation, then the *Dun and Bradstreet Reports* of unlisted companies can be used for preliminary financial data.

Once the data is obtained, then the preliminary financial analysis should be made. The data to be collected should include a list of the products as well as the trends in recent years. Balance sheets and income statements are very important since these provide analysis of assets such as cash position of the firm, receivables balance, inventories, etc.

FINANCIAL ANALYSIS

The financial analysis of the company should incorporate a comparative price analysis of the seller versus that of the buyer. Market performance of the stock over the last five years, including EPS, stock market value, and price earning ratio should be evaluated. It is always essential in the preliminary evaluation process to collect other than financial information about the candidate. Such information will include: (1) a history and background, (2) a general description of the firm's present business, and (3) a list of competitors and their geographical locations. In analyzing what the buyer should pay for the acquisition candidate, several points must be considered.

1. Evaluation of net worth of the firm must be done in light of the inventory and depreciation methods used. The net worth method may not be a good measure of a manufacturing business, but rather may be good for such organizations as a bank or other type of service firms.

2. Market value may be utilized to appraise the physical assets as well as other intangibles of the firm.

3. Competitors' current price earning ratio may he used as a guide in determining the acquisition candidate's market price per share.

Once the acquisition's preliminary financial analysis is complete, the facts regarding the candidate should be summarized and an outline of the advantages and disadvantages of the acquisition should be prepared.

If, based on the preliminary financial analysis, the result is positive and the decision is to go ahead, then a detailed financial analysis should follow. This financial investigation should then determine the accuracy and fairness of the financial data used as well as the appropriate accounting method that must be used for such an acquisition.

ACQUISITION METHOD

In reviewing the financial statement of the acquisition candidate, the staff responsible for the review should carefully look at the accounting method that should be used. There are two basic alternative methods for handling an acquisition transaction. These are (1) purchase and (2) pooling of interest. They apply to all acquisitions whether achieved through an asset acquisition or a stock acquisition. However, the "pooling of interest" was ruled out by the Financial Accounting Standard Board (FASB). According to FASB Statement No. 141 transactions initiated after June 30, 2001, must use the purchase method of accounting for business combinations. The provisions in FASB Statement No. 141 reflect a different approach than what was discussed in Opinion No. 16. According to FASB No. 141, the single method approach used reflects the conclusion that all business combinations are acquisitions and should be accounted for in the same way under a single method – the purchase method. [1]

Purchase Method: In this type of method, the acquired firm is treated as an investment by the acquirer. The excess in price paid by the acquirer over and above the net worth of the firm being acquired is recorded as goodwill. This goodwill, according to FASB Statement No. 142, should be initially recognized as an asset in the financial statements and measured as the excess of the cost of an acquisition. It should be assigned to reporting units of the acquiring entity that is supposed to benefit from the synergies of the merger and amortized over 15 years for tax purposes beginning with the month in which the intangible is recognized according to Section 197 of the IRC. Positive goodwill should be avoided, if possible, because it will have a negative impact on future earnings. However, if the price paid by the acquirer is below the net worth of the firm acquired, then "negative goodwill"[2] is generated. This type of goodwill does not truly exist as an accounting terminology, but the amount it represents is used to reduce non-current assets, thus generating an impact on future earnings.

Pooling of Interest: This popular method of accounting was ruled out by FASB since all mergers/business combinations are now accounted for under the purchase method of accounting. Prior to this ruling the pooling-of-interest method was very popular. Under this method, the acquirer combines the book value of the acquired firm's assets and liabilities with its own. The paid-in capital of the acquired firm is assigned to the securities issued by the acquirer. In addition, the retained earnings of the acquired firm is added to that of the acquirer. In other terms, the assets and liabilities are added, and as a result, the goodwill is not reflected in the "business combination," which would reflect no change in business income. However, if a Not for Profit organization is acquiring a for Profit company, the Not for Profit organization can still use the pooling method in the business combination process. See FASB Statement 141 for details relative to the revised status of this method of accounting as used in business combinations. [3]

EPS

In the past the earning per share calculation used in the preliminary financial review was calculated utilizing either of these accounting methods. However, the pooling-of-interest

---

1 "Summary of Statement No. 141" Financial Accounting Standard Board, AICPA. June 2001. 12 August 2002. http://www.fasb.org/st/summary/stsum141.shtml
2 In the finance and accouting literature, there is no such term as "negative goodwill." Usually, the difference between the purchase price and the net worth is used in this case to reduce non-current assets. The reason the author utilizes the term "negative goodwill" is to assist the practitioner in comprehending the concepts involved in a purchase transaction.
3 "Summary of Statement No. 141" Financial Accounting Standard Board, AICPA. June 2001. 12 August 2002. http://www.fasb.org/st/summary/stsum141.shtml

method was only permissible whenever the twelve criteria stated by the FASB were met. Furthermore, if the acquisition did not qualify for pooling of interest, then the purchase method had to be used. The impact on EPS was a factor that determined the accounting method the firm wants to use since the financial consequences of the purchase versus pooling-of-interest methods would be indicative of which direction the firm should take, especially if the firm is publicly owned and management is concerned about the amount of the EPS that should be reported to the stockholders.

FINANCIAL REPORTS & POLICIES REQUIRED

The process to be followed in the detailed financial review should be based on obtaining the following financial reports:

1. Audited balance sheets and operating statements for the past five years.

2. Current backlog of orders with comparable figures for at least one year prior to the investigation for such an acquisition.

3. Detailed sales and cost of sales by product line for at least two years.

4. Detailed sales and cost of sales by channel of distribution for at least two years, preferably five years if available.

5. Accounts and notes receivables-credit policy and aging analysis; current figures if available.

6. Inventory summary in dollars for (a) raw material, (b) goods in process and (c) finished goods.

7. Method of valuing inventories, (i.e.) Last-in, First-out; First-in, First-out; Average.

8. Inventory policies and practice used with regard to warranty, obsolete material and slow-moving items.

9. Brief statement of depreciation policies, bad debts and date of the latest physical inventory.

10. Comments of any unusual charges such as royalties received, interest payments, capital gains, etc. shown under other income and other deductions.

11. Schedules of any important contractual agreement such as employment contracts/material purchase contracts.

12. Tabulation of overall company employment showing number of employees, direct and indirect hourly labor, fringe benefits, pension plan and employees' stock option plan, if there is one in effect.

13. Contractual agreements given by top management, if any.

14. Brief summary of litigation during the past five years which might have yielded loss/gain to the company. Also any litigation still pending.

15. The firm's best projection for the next five years of sales and profits. Identify if forecast includes new products.

16. List of new products and the amount of sales and profits included in the forecast. If any, estimate of major capital expenditure for achieving the increased sales volume should be indicated.

ANALYSIS PROCEDURES

In the balance sheet analysis process, the liabilities should be analyzed. The possibility of unrecorded liabilities must be clarified because often medium-sized and smaller firms are not precise about reflecting all liabilities in their financial statements other than at fiscal year end. This can be determined by a comparative analysis of the current period with previously audited periods. However, in the case of Enron, this could not have been detected since the equities in the partnerships were recorded while the portion of the liabilities were not reflected except in a footnote which was shown in a very small print. Auditors should not allow such a practice to take place, but the Houston office of Arthur Anderson which oversaw the auditing of Enron's books was investigated by the United States Congress since the documents were destroyed after the SEC began an inquiry into Enron's accounting practices according to the *Wall Street Journal* series of articles that were published in the January 22,23, and 24, 2002 issues. These practices along with others at WorldCom and Tyco were not in line with General Accepted Accounting Principles (GAAP) which lead to the establishment of The Sarbanes-Oxley Act that was signed into law by President George W. Bush in 2002. Such an act was passed to help elimininate the deception of stakeholders as well as assist top management in making ethical and justifiable decisions.

Inquiry should be made as to the status of federal and state income tax matters; for example, a company's prior year tax returns should be examined and the result of the examination should be compared to the current year's practices. If deficiency assessment has existed in prior periods, it is possible that it may exist in the current period/year. This, in fact, should assist the analyst in calculating any pending tax liability.

Expenditures for legal and other expenses should be reviewed. Inquiry regarding the company premises must be made; if the premises involve substantial rentals, a search should be made to determine whether the premises are owned by an affiliated firm or if long-term lease agreement would result in a legal question in the event of a business combination.

The income statement and the balance sheet of the buyer and that of the firm to be acquired should be summarized on a comparable accounting basis for a period of five years prior to the current year and for five projected years, including the current period. If the firm being acquired has been in existence for less than five years, then the comparative financial consolidation should be structured for the life of the acquisition candidate. Accounting adjustments should be made to conform with that of the acquirer's accounting practice. Adjustments may he needed in the areas of inventory valuation, depreciation, tool amortization, deferred research expense, goodwill, reserves dealing with vacation pay, etc., and federal tax reserves.

Once the data is collected, audited, and transcribed in the acquirer's format, then the calculation for the purchase price should be made. There are various approaches for determining the candidate's purchase price. These approaches are discussed in Part Three (3), Chapter 8, in detail.

Although the financial analysis did not specify the type of financing the company should take, it nevertheless covered the most important aspect of the analysis process. However, the effect on the buyer's debt ratio is important. Therefore, the calculation should include different types of financing (i.e.) debt, equity, or a combination of both. Hence, any method chosen would create a financial impact on the EPS. Details of these financing methods will be discussed in Chapter 8.

As stated earlier, an acquisition of a company by a buyer would create a divestment to the seller. How a seller can, therefore, evaluate a divestment is the subject of Chapter 6.

CHAPTER 6

DIVESTMENT EVALUATION AND THE FIRM'S PLAN

What does Lovejoy's definition of "divestment" assume?

What is the difference between a voluntary divestment and an involuntary divestment?

What are some common reasons for divestment?

What items help to determine a divestment candidate?

How is divestment considered in longrange planning?

As stated in Chapter 1, divestment is a process of eliminating a portion of an enterprise while looking for a secure way to maintain or improve the current profit position of a company. Assets that are underutilized should not be tolerated by a firm, because such assets may begin showing a negative financial impact on the organization under analysis. A common approach is a thorough analysis of working capital and fixed assets which is usually prompted by the heavy demand for capital funds needed for investment opportunities that might yield a higher return on investment. In choosing the approach to be followed, the decision is influenced by the long-range plan of the firm under study. In this chapter, the following items are covered:

1. Divestment as defined in literature versus that of the practical definition expressed in Chapter 1.

2. Groups of divestments.

3. Reasons that are valid in a divestment process.

4. Methods of recognizing divestment candidates.

5. Long-range planning and the divestment Process.

DEFINITION

Financial writers have seemingly avoided the term divestment. Although divestments took place prior to the '70's, the term was not generally used in the finance literature. Frederick Lovejoy introduced his book in 1971, which he called Divestment for Profit. Lovejoy defined divestment as:

> "... the Process of eliminating a portion of the enterprise and the subsequent use of the resources which are freed for some other purposes. A divestment takes place when there is a disposal of company assets, as well as a discontinuance of an activity which has been associated with those assets. Thus, divestment occurs when there is a complete cessation of a part of the enterprise and the disposition of some, or all, of the facilities connected with by sale, transfer, destruction or gift." [1]

According to Lovejoy, divestment works on the assumption that management would continue to operate the remaining part of the business. This can be illustrated by the approach taken

---

[1] Federick A. Lovejoy, *Divestment for Profit* (New York, N.Y.: Financial Executives Research Foundation, 1971), p. 3.

by International Telephone and Telegraph Corporation (ITT) since the retirement of Harold S. Geneen as Chairman and Chief Executive Officer. ITT started its disacquisition process in January of 1979; the 24 billion-dollar-in-sales corporation divested and shut down about thirtythree of its companies and divisional operations which yielded approximately $1 billion in revenue annually. However, ITT continued to improve its operation.[2] Observers wonder: Why the divestment approach and in what group of divestments would these thirty-three operations be considered?

DIVESTMENT GROUPS

Divestments are not always composed of unprofitable subsidiaries and divisions. They can be profitable product lines, sections of operations, and a total line of business. All the divestments fall into one of the following groups:

1. Voluntary Divestment.

2. Involuntary Divestment.

Voluntary Divestment - takes place when management decides to divest a portion of the company either because it is unprofitable or because management objectives demand such an action for reinvestment purposes. However, management's intention to divest can vary and cash flow may be one of its intentions. For example, a portion of the National Education Corporation acquisition of Intext, Incorporated was financed through debt which resulted in the subsequent divestment of Haddon Craftsmen and other operations in order to generate the immediate cash flow for debt reduction. In other words, financing an acquisition by borrowing increases the debt ratio and may jeopardize a company's credit rating. Therefore, an immediate divestment of a portion of the firm results in a positive cash flow that can be used to reduce the debt -- thus bringing down the debt ratio to the level prior to the acquisition. This can also be illustrated by the acquisition of additional shares in DBA by the Bendix Corporation which shifted Bendix ownership from a little over 50% to approximately 94% ownership. The intention was to use a combination of debt and equity financing and later divest profitable operations such as Roto Diesel and others to yield the required cash flow needed to reduce the debt ratio to approximately its original figure.

Divestments in this group can be either a sale of stock or a liquidation of a total operation. The corporate financial analysis would really determine the direction the corporation should follow in its divestment approach.

Involuntary Divestments - are required by Federal or state agencies for various reasons which most commonly involve the area of restrictions of competition. For example, after the Bendix Corporation's acquisition of Fram and Autolite, the FTC determined that unfair

---

2 ITT: Groping for a New Strategy," *BusinessWeek*, December 15, 1980, p. 66

competition may be created in the automotive market by Bendix. It forced Bendix to divest some of the operations which compelled Bendix into establishing the Facet Enterprises, Inc. This was later divested through a spin-off process with its own stockholders of approximately 27,400. Another example is the forcing of International Business Machines (IBM) to divest the Service Bureau Corporation.

In other cases, the divestment can be forced on a corporation if it fails to pay its debt-thus resulting in a bankruptcy which means that the corporation should liquidate its assets and pay its debt. In this situation, three or more creditors with claims in excess of $500 initiate the action by filing a petition with the court. However, if the total number of creditors is less than twelve, any one creditor can file a petition.

REASONS FOR DIVESTMENT

There can be several reasons for divestment as stated earlier. These reasons can easily express the importance of divestment. Common reasons for divestment are as follows:

1. Corporate objectives of improved profits.

2. Corporate cash needs.

3. Better opportunities for investment.

4. Change in management as well as a change in corporate objectives.

5. Justice Department requirements and FTC rulings.

If improved profits is a reason for divestment, why do acquisitions come first? The basic objective is the improvement of profits in both acquisitions and divestments. As in the ITT example stated earlier, the ITT driving factor for selling off thirty-three operations was the sluggish profits that the company experienced over the periods prior to 1979. Mr. Rand V. Araskog, ITT Chief Executive Officer during 1980 expressed the following concern, according to Business Week:

> "Two factors are driving these sell-offs. Sluggish profits for the past five years have pushed ITT to rid itself mainly of poor performers. But a second, less recognized factor weighs equally heavily. The future of ITT's main business, telecommunications equipment, is fraught with some awesome risks, partly be cause the company has been losing

> ground in a technological revolution. Both problems mean
> that ITT must trim itself to fight for improvement.".[3]

Companies tend to divest when they are unable to support a capital base, thus getting rid of very profitable operations. This can be exemplified by Esmark, Incorporated divesting one of its most profitable operations, the Wickes Energy Corporation. This divestiture was based upon Wickes cash needs to finance the energy operation's future growth which Esmark, Inc. felt could not be easily supported without making other operations (within its corporate structure) suffer a capital shortage.[4] Although this reason for divestment can be one aspect of cash needs, another may deal with divestment to raise cash and reduce expensive debt that might be negatively impacting the corporate EPS.

Frequently, the divestment is for the purpose of investment opportunities elsewhere. This reason can identify the mastermind executives who try to implement such a strategy. A successful implementation has been demonstrated by Mr. William Sneath, Chairman of the Board of Union Carbide. Mr. Sneath tried to channel investment funds into the core operations of Union Carbide. His strategic approach is clearly stated in his statement "…we are concentrating on what we do best and that means channeling investment funds to our core business."[5]

Whatever the reason or the corporate strategy might be, it is always management's philosophy that seeks to justify the divestment if the divestment is not due to poor profit performance. Management generally follows the trend. In this type of economy, divestment may be the result of rationalization of the deployment of resources. Therefore, management may seek to concentrate its resources in the highest return business sector and yet the lowest risk. Management has the tendency to follow this approach rather than to diversify the company's operations inprofitable sectors that might be high return and high risk. Management seems to pursue this goal in the 80's by divesting itself of subsidiaries and divisions that do not fit the corporate objectives even though they may be profitable. An example of this is Bendix's divestment of American Forest Products and the attempt to utilize the cash in other acquisitions which would complement the Aerospace industry. Mr. William Agee, former Chairman and Chief Executive Officer of the Bendix Corporation, was trying to adopt the concept of the rationalization of the deployment of resources. He would have succeeded in acquiring Martin Marietta Corporation had the Bendix staff working on the project carefully planned the implementation of such a strategy.

---

3   ITT: Groping for a New Strategy," op. cit., p. 66.
4   Lynn Adkins, "Divestitures: A New Business Rage," *Dun's Review*, March 1981, p. 113
5   "Back to Basics," *The Economist Newspaper*, LTD., May 2, 1981, p. 74.

METHODS OF RECOGNIZING DIVESTMENT CANDIDATES

The technique used for locating divestment candidates varies from company to company. If an evaluation of the performance of a subsidiary/division reflects substandard performance, it indicates that further study is needed. Past performance may not be a time indicator of future performance; however, reporting techniques that provide early detection often aid in recognizing candidates for divestiture. For example, corporate implementation of quarterly financial reviews, as well as annual review meetings, can be the basis for recognizing a divestiture candidate. These financial reviews may result in an in-depth study of a division or subsidiary, thus asking divisional top management for further financial data, including a five-year history.

In most cases, top management establishes warning signs such as hurdle rates or financial ratios that point out the need for additional investigation. These rates can be cutoff rates utilized in ranking divestment candidates. The following criteria should be considered when evaluating divestment candidates:

1. Evaluation of past, present, and future projected performance of a product, division or subsidiary.

2. Analysis of funds generated from operation and funds required by the operation.

3. Impact of continued operation on EPS and cash flow position as well as the debt ratio of the corporation.

4. Impact of divestment on the EPS and the cash flow position as well as the debt ratio of the corporation.

5. Analysis of ROA, ROI, internal rate of return (IRR) and return on sales (ROS) for each Product, division or subsidiary in question.

6. Comparative analysis of the ratios in the preceding item with that of the average industry and other corporate operation.

7. Analysis of the liquidity position using the Current Ratio which is equal to

$$\frac{\textit{Current Assets}}{\textit{Current Liabilities}}$$

and the Acid-Test Ratio which is equal to

$$\frac{Current\ Assets - Inventories}{Current\ Liabilities}$$

Comparative analysis of these ratios for subsidiaries with that of the average industry is recommended.

8. List of remedies available for improvement of profit performance and the financial impact that these remedies will have on the corporate EPS, ROA, ROI, ROS, IRR and cash flow position.

The determination of the order of divestment (if more than one is in question) should be made according to the preceding items listed. A schedule of the financial factors should be structured and these factors must be used in the ranking process. This method is clearly illustrated in Chapter 12, Part Four, of this text.

LONG-RANGE PLANNING AND THE DIVESTMENT PROCESS

Divestment should be part of the corporate long-range plan. It should provide answers to questions that should be raised by top management. These questions would include the following:

1. Is a given product contributing adequate sales and profits to the corporation? How would future technology impact the sales and profits of such a product?

2. Is a given division/subsidiary performance in line with the required corporate rate of return? What are the prospects that such a division or subsidiary will have the same performance in the future?

3. Is the line of business under review causing a drain on company's profit and cash? Will it be causing the same impact in the future?

4. Does the company intend to diversify and how would these products, divisions, or subsidiaries under review fit into the corporate plan?

5. What other opportunities does the corporation have to utilize the funds from such a divestiture? If opportunities are available, what rate of return will be realized?

In considering a divestment, corporate planners must review the occurrence of extraordinary items on the corporate long-range plan. Such items may generate a favorable or unfavorable impact on corporate funds. They include (1) separation payments, (2) pension settlement,

(3) write-off of goodwill, and (4) profit/loss from the divestiture of the business. These items, as well as the corporate policies, must he considered in the corporate long-range planning of divestment. Illustrations and analytical examples of the divestment are covered in Chapters 12 and 13, Part Four of this text.

CHAPTER 7

RELATED STATUTORY LAWS VERSUS SECURITIES AND EXCHANGE LAWS

What are "blue-sky" laws?

What is the Uniform Securities Act?

What is a pre-notification report to the SEC and when is it required?

As stated in Chapter 3, the filing of notification for "acquisitions and divestments" is required by the U.S. Anti-Trust agencies such as the SEC and the FTC. However, exemptions from pre-acquisition notification may exist depending on the nature of the acquisition as specified in Chapter 3, pages 14 and 15.

The FTC implemented the 7A section of the Clayton Act which became effective on September 5, 1978. This section requires that the acquirer must file a pre-acquisition notification with the FTC and wait for a period of 30 days before consummating the acquisition.

The filing procedure must be done with the Anti-Trust Division of the Department of Justice and the FTC. Notification forms entitled "anti-trust improvement act notification and reports" must be filed on time. This type of notification would include (1) transaction description, (2) acquisition contract, and (3) accounting records regarding the candidate's evaluation.

Although notifications and information must be filed with both the FTC and SEC, the SEC differs from the FTC in that the SEC through its Washington, D.C. office makes public information filed with the SEC available to the public. In other words, any individual can visit the SEC public room in Washington, D.C. and review any pre-acquisition notification or stock purchase agreement of any publicly held company. However, if the person/company wishes to receive the information by mail, it can be available for a nominal fee. This information service is available through Disclosure, which is part of Thomson Financial, and works very closely with the SEC in meeting public request for disclosure of information. However, disclosure of information is currently available on-line for a fee through a database system provided by Disclosure, Bethesda, Maryland. Furthermore, a person seeking free information may be able to access it through Edgar archives at www.sec.gov/.

The history of the anti-trust laws which started in 1890 with the Sherman Anti-Trust Act has led to the current SEC disclosure.

STATUTORY VS. SEC LAWS

Before 1933, regulations of the securities were restricted to state security laws. There were no federal security laws until 1933. Today, the SEC has a major control over the issuance and trading of securities. It cooperates closely with federal, state, and local law enforcement agencies in preventing security fraud. State laws dealing with fraud prevention are commonly known as bluesky laws. These blue-sky laws have different provisions which encompass the following: (1) special functions of the Office of the Secretary of State to administer organization and corporate mergers, (2) requirements for licensing of securities firms, (3) listed standards to obtain official clearance before offering of securities begin, (4) filing of accounting and financial data relative to a request for additional issue, and (5) criteria for defining and administering security fraud as well as determining the penalties associated with the fraud committed.

To illustrate the statutory laws, let's look at the Commonwealth of Pennsylvania (Pa.) Laws. Both the SEC and the Commonwealth of Pa. require the registration of securities and insist upon strict compliance with the laws of "full disclosure" of facts relating to a security and its issuing corporation. Under the Commonwealth of Pa. Corporation Laws, Section 201 of the 1972 Act, as amended, it is unlawful for any individual to offer securities for sale in the State unless (a) the security is registered or (b) the security is exempt. Exemption of the securities under the Commonwealth of Pennsylvania applies to the following:

1. Securities issued or guaranteed by the United States (U.S.) and any other American State, including the Canadian Province.

2. Securities of banks and savings associations.

3. Securities guaranteed by credit unions.

4. Securities of educational, religious, social or charitable organizations.

5. Securities that are approved by the New York Stock Exchange, or any of the national security exchanges.

6. Securities of registered broker-dealer issued to its officers, partners or employees.

7. Securities issued in connection with employees' stock option plans.

8. Securities which the Commonwealth does not find necessary for protection of investors.

Various sections of the Pennsylvania 1972 Act, as amended, regarding the Pa. Business Corporation and the issuance of securities, clearly covers prerequisites for foreign corporations regarding registration requirements. For example, Section 206 requires foreign corporations to register with the Pa. Bureau of Corporation which involves the process of registering securities by qualification. There can be at least two ways of offering securities under Section 206. These ways include, but are not limited to, the following:

1. Interstate offering made pursuant to the exemption encompassed in Section 3 (a) (11) of the 1933 Securities Act and private offerings made pursuant to the exemption contained in 4 (2) of the same Act.

2. Non-exempt securities registered twenty days before they are publicly offered and fully supported with registration statement filed with the SEC containing detailed information concerning legal, technological and financial position of the issuer.

The state laws go beyond the controlling of securities. They preserve the right of the seller's stockholders' monetary recovery if the buyer has not complied with the Commonwealth of Pa. laws. Furthermore, state laws have become very strict regarding acquisitions made by foreign corporations. The state has the right to block such an acquisition if the transaction is an asset transaction which has not had prior shareholders' approval of that of the seller.

The approval must be obtained at the shareholders' meeting which is called for the purpose of considering such a sale. However, if the transaction is a takeover bid and not an asset acquisition, the laws in most states require that certain information he filed with the Securities and Exchange Commission prior to the time of making it a tender offer. This can be further illustrated by the attempted takeover of Martin Marietta Corporation (a Maryland Corporation) by the Bendix corporation (a Delaware Corporation) and vice versa.[1]

Uniformity of Blue-Sky Laws: As stated earlier, blue-sky laws are not identical, but most states have provisions for (1) fraud in the sale of securities, (2) registration of securities, and (3) registration of dealers-brokers and investment advisers and salespersons. However, what makes the corporation laws at the state level somewhat similar is the Uniform Securities Act on Uniform State laws which was approved on August 25, 1956, and was amended a few times since then. This act consists of four parts of which the first three parts represent the three basic blue-sky laws. These three parts include: (1) fraud, (2) registration of broker-dealer agents, and (3) registration of securities. Part four covers general provisions which are an important supplement to the first three basic parts. Some of these supplementary provisions include: (1) definition of terms, (2) exemptions, (3) judicial review, (4) investigatory, (5) criminal, etc.

The Uniform Securities Act, as amended, has been partially or fully adopted by approximately thirty-four states in addition to the District of Columbia, Puerto Rico, and the US Virgin Islands. These states are: (1) Alabama, (2) Alaska, (3) Arkansas, (4) Colorado, (5) Delaware, (6) Hawaii, (7) Idaho, (8) Indiana, (9) Iowa) (10) Kansas, (11) Kentucky, (12) Maine, (13) Maryland, (14) Massachusetts, (15) Michigan, (16) Minnesota, (17) Missouri, (18) Montana, (19) Nebraska, (20) Nevada, (21) New Jersey, (22) New Mexico, (23) Oklahoma, (24) Oregon, (25) Pennsylvania, (26) South Carolina, (27) South Dakota, (28) Utah, (29) Vermont, (30) Virginia, (31) Washington, (32) West Virginia, (33) Wisconsin, and (34) Wyoming.

---

1   *Reference is made to The Wall Street Journal of August 31, 1982 and The New York Times, Business Day Setion of August 31, as well as September 2, 1983. In addition, the Schedules 14D- 1 filed with the SEC by both the Bendix Corporation and Marietta Corporation..*

RELATED STATUTORY LAWS VERSUS SECURITIES AND EXCHANGE LAWS

SEC and State Laws Regarding Takeovers and Mergers: A "takeover," as defined in Chapter 1, is a tender offer to buy securities by making a direct bid to the stockholders of the seller despite the opposition of seller's management. In other words, the buyer in such a transaction is attempting to acquire a percentage of ownership in excess of that allowed by the Securities and Exchange Act of 1934 as amended by the William Bill of July, 1968.

The William Bill outlines the procedure that must be followed in making a tender offer or an attempted takeover. The procedure requires the acquiring corporation to file with the SEC information in the format described in Schedules 13G and 14D-1, shown in Appendix B.

This procedure can be illustrated by the Martin Marietta's Corporation tender offer bid to the Common stockholders of the Bendix Corporation.[2] The offer was to purchase for cash up to 11,900,000 shares of the common stock of the Bendix Corporation at seventy-five ($75) dollars per share. The proration period was to expire at 12:00 midnight, New York City time, Thursday, September 21, 1982. Such a submission (based on the Schedule 14D-1 is shown in Appendix B of this text) included the terms of the offer, the number of shares, the payment of the purchase price, the withdrawal rights, the tax consequences to the shareholders, i.e. taxable transaction, the procedure for tendering the shares, the price range of shares as well as policy regarding announced dividends, the financial data on Bendix as well as Martin Marietta, the sources and amount of funds for the acquisition, the background of the offer, the purpose of the offer, the effect of the offer on market for the shares, the stock exchange listings, the extension of the tender offer, the termination of the tender offer, legal implications, and fees and expenses.

In this submission, it is evident that Martin Marietta was aware of the state laws and therefore made the statement on page 14 of the document that the offer was being made without compliance by Martin Marietta with certain takeover statutes that may purport to apply to the offer. The blue-sky laws in Delaware, Michigan, New Jersey, and Missouri were set to protect the stockholders who have placed their trust in the State of Delaware for granting the Bendix Charter as well as the trust in the other states where Bendix has filed qualification to do business by opening manufacturing plants and service offices.

Martin Marietta's proposal to acquire Bendix was generated by Bendix's tender offer to acquire Martin Marietta. The Bendix Corporation submission on August 30, 1982 of additional pre-merger notification report with the Securities and Exchange was in line with the Hart-ScottRodino Anti-Trust Improvement Act. The filing under this Act would permit Bendix to acquire in its tender offer more than fifty percent (50%) of Martin Marietta's share. On page 14 of the Bendix Schedule 14D-1 submission, the purpose of the offer was to acquire approximately forty-four and a half percent (44.5%) held by Bendix. However,

---

2 *"Schedule 14D-1 - Tender Offer Statement Pursuant to Section 14(d) (1) of the Securities Exchange Act of 1934" filed by Martin Marietta Corporation with the Securities and Exchange Commission, Washington, D.C., September 2, pp. 1-184*

Bendix's management intention was to acquire all the remaining outstanding shares through merger between Martin Marietta and a subsidiary of Bendix.[3]

The attempt by Bendix's management was first to acquire control through a cash transaction estimated at $690 million, financed mostly through short-term revolving credit by approximately a total of nineteen (19) domestic and foreign banks. Once this was achieved, Bendix's management would have owned approximately fifty percent (50%) --thus being able to cast their voting shares in favor of the merger. Under Maryland state law and in line with the Martin Marietta's charter, a merger requires the prior approval of the majority of the stockholders. This approach, if successful, would have placed Bendix in no violation of state laws since prior to the time of the merger, the Bendix Corporation could have been entitled to vote, thus forming any or all dissenters to accent the strategic plan under Maryland law. In this attempt, the Bendix plan had carefully considered the Maryland blue-sky law, even to the point of calling a special meeting for electing new board members, since under the Maryland state law the holders of twenty-five percent (25%) or more of the shares have the right to call a special meeting for the purpose of removing company directors or filling vacancies on the board of directors.

SEC REGISTRATION, FILING AND REVIEW PROCEDURE

A corporation intending to issue stock must make sure that investors get all the information they need to know regarding the security issue. Therefore, the corporation must file a registration statement with the SEC containing financial information as well as detailed information on the issuing corporation. These requirements are in line with the Securities Act of 1933. It is imperative that the supplementary information filed with the registration statement be cleared by the SEC prior to the sale of any securities. The information required is clearly defined in SEC Rule 405, which states that the information required must be important to a reasonable investor who, based on the information, would determine whether or not to purchase the securities registered.

In addition to registration requirement for additional issue of securities, the SEC requires corporations to file pre-notification reports with the SEC if the corporation intends to obtain more than five percent (5%) of another company's equity securities. This pre-notification can be achieved by filing Schedules 13G and 14D-1. Copies of these schedules with special instructions are shown in Appendix B. As illustrated earlier in the case of Bendix and Martin Marietta, the corporation is expected to complete 14D-1 in compliance with the requirements of Section 13 (d) of the Securities Exchange Act of 1934. The instructions for filing this schedule and the utilization of the information required is presented in Appendix B. Eight copies of this Schedule along with all exhibits and supplementary information must

---

3 "Schedule 14D-1 - Tender Offer Statement Pursuant to Section 14(d) (1) of the Securities Exchange Act of 1934," filed by the Bendix Corporation with the Securities and Exchange Commission, Washington, D.C., August 26, 1982, pp. 1-706

be filed with the SEC. Since filing fees may change, it is advisable that the corporation filing the Schedule call the SEC office in Washington, D.C. for the current filing fee. If the acquirer decides to terminate a tender offer, it must promptly file a final amendment to Schedule 14D-1, with the SEC, outlining all changes and stating that the tender-offer has been terminated.

Another schedule referred to as Schedule 13D can be filed with the SEC. Six copies of this should be filed, if the filing person has previously filed a statement on Schedule 13G to report the acquisition which is the subject of Schedule 13D complying with Rule 13d 1(b) 3 or 4. The information required to be filed with this schedule 13D shall be deemed necessary in line with sections of the 1934 Act and all its provisions. A copy of this schedule along with the instruction is shown in Appendix C.

This filing procedure can be exemplified by the Bendix Corporation filing of Schedules 13G, and 14D-1 for the tender-offer made to the Martin Marietta stockholders. In addition, Bendix's submission of schedule 13D on December 30, 1982 expressing Allied Corporation's interest in Bendix stock should be reviewed. The supplementary information to this Schedule 13D included the following: (1) identity and background, (2) purpose of the transaction, (3) interest in securities of the issuer, (4) contract arrangements, and (5) exhibits of stock purchase agreement with updated amendments. The signature of the Vice-president, Secretary and General Counsel is placed, testifying that after reasonable inquiry and to the best of its knowledge and belief that it certifies that the information set forth in this statement is true, complete and correct. A copy of the first five pages of this submission is included in Appendix C for the benefit of the reader.

In reviewing the SEC laws versus that of statutory laws, illustration was given on Bendix and Martin Marietta Corporations, covering takeover problems with regard to these laws. Also, publicity by both corporations and counter-takeover bid by Martin Marietta (the Pac Man Defense) were discussed in light of the filing requirements set forth in the William Bill of July 1968. The possible defensive litigation by Bendix regarding the strategic merger of Martin Marietta after the acquisition was illustrated by showing the Bendix plan in line with Maryland statutory laws.

Acquisitions, whether stock or asset, therefore, must meet statutory laws. Chapters 8 and 9 cover the procedural steps by which a corporation would be able to identify the candidate and how the negotiation would proceed.

PART THREE

Acquisition Procedure

CHAPTER 8

CANDIDATE IDENTIFICATION AND PURCHASE PRICE DETERMINATION

What may be the goals of the acquirer in seeking an acquisition?

What might be the effect of diversification?

What are three ways of increasing earnings per share (EPS) that a company might consider?

What factors in the business environment might influence the choice of a potential candidate for acquisition?

What are some of the screening criteria for selecting a potential acquisition candidate?

What techniques should be used to contact a potential acquisition candidate?

What are the five ways of determining the purchase price of a company?

How can an acquisition be financed?

In an acquisition process, the acquirer should seek to know the business of the prospective candidate as well as knowing his own business. How the prospective candidate can be identified is the subject of this chapter.

ACQUIRER'S GOAL

It is essential that the acquirer outline his goals and objectives. If the acquirer intends to ensure the continuation of his own business, then the acquisition candidate may be a competitor. Or, the acquisition may be for the sole maximization of EPS and this may open the horizon of the search. That is, the acquirer may be looking at operations and product lines that are in a different line of business. This will no doubt initiate a diversification strategy which would involve risk and profitability, depending on the amount of maximization of EPS the acquirer is targeting for his company. The acquirer should review the possibility of diversification based on two basic elements:

1. The logic of flexibility of resources and the potential loss of cost advantage due to diversification.

2. The ability and flexibility of the acquirer's management to deal with innovation other than the familiar business situation they are in.

TRADE-OFFS ON GOALS AND OBJECTIVES

As stated earlier, the acquirer should have a long-range plan outlining the goals and objectives of the corporation. He should look for a business with which he is knowledgeable. The acquirer should study his own business and determine its capabilities and drawbacks. This study should include the review of the acquirer's manufacturing methods, personnel qualifications, cash, and sales capabilities. Based on this review, a list of criteria for candidate selections should be structured. This list of criteria may result in the trade-offs among various criteria which the acquirer may use in choosing the candidate for study. This means that as one criterion wins, another one may lose. Recognition of these trade-offs among various criteria is important in determining the final check list of goals and objectives needed for the targeted area of business in which an acquisition candidate would be selected.

As an example, consider a corporation such as Bendix, which is in the aerospace and automotive lines of business, and suppose it has a primary goal of increasing its EPS by twenty-five percent (25%). There are different alternatives to achieve the targeted increase through acquisition, but trade-offs of criteria may be necessary for goal achievement. Let us consider three different strategies for acquisitions by Bendix for the purpose of increasing EPS.

1. Bendix can further diversify its operation into computer technology by acquiring Apple or Dell.

2. Bendix can acquire supplementary product lines.

3. Bendix can acquire a company in its own strong lines of business (i.e.) aerospace or automotive.

Each of these aforementioned alternatives implies a different operating strategy for the Bendix Corporation, yet each alternative may allow Bendix to arrive at an identical overall targeted EPS.

In diversification, emphasis may be placed on minimizing risk yet seeking a line of business where the expertise would be entrusted in the acquired managerial and technical staff. However, this procedure would expose the acquiring corporation to the risk of losing the acquired highly technical staff. Furthermore, the alternative of supplementary product lines may assist in increased sales as a result of improved market share due to a strategic move against competitors who manufacture/sell the same product lines but not its supplement. This would achieve targeted EPS; however, economic situations negatively impacting the existing product lines would have a direct negative impact on the newly acquired products-- thus decreasing the chance for an EPS increase of twenty-five percent (25%).

The alternative of acquiring a candidate in the same line of business of either aerospace or automotive may give the right support based on the assumption that the Bendix management along with the research and development staff are competent in their field and can successfully improve the acquired operation to achieve the targeted EPS.

The trade-offs criteria in selecting the line of business can vary based on corporate objectives. In summary, it can be diversification vs. the risk of remaining in the same line of business. Yet the risk in diversification due to acquirer's managerial skills may exist. Therefore, the trade-offs of goals and objectives would depend on the degree of risk that the acquirer is willing to take.

IDENTIFICATION OF POTENTIAL CANDIDATES

In the determination process, the acquirer must first study his current and expected future performance. Evaluation of the total market expansion and stability over the next five to ten years is extremely important. The projected future report should include an evaluation of each product line, the overall line of business, current and future competition, acquirer's past performance, and the product pricing policy as well as the industry trends.

In addition, the acquirer must consider the business environment. Factors impacting the business environment would include:

1. Interest rates and idle cash.

2. FTC regulations.

3. Stock market prices.

4. Tax implications based on the sections of the Code impacting the acquisition.

In Chapter 1, pages 5, 6, 7, and 8, a discussion of "why acquire?" explained that the acquisition may be intended for corporate growth which can be classified as either vertical, horizontal, or conglomerate. The source for a potential candidate, therefore, can be determined by the classification of the acquisition. If the acquisition is "vertical" or "horizontal" the acquirer's own employees can be the first source for identifying a list of candidates, since the acquirer's employees would be familiar with their suppliers as well as their competitors.

If the acquisition is classified as "conglomerate," then the acquirer should utilize brokerage firms and pay the required finder's fee in the case of successful acquisition transaction. Regardless of the acquisition's classification, a major source of information can be the acquirer's board of directors. The board of directors may have insight into potential successful candidates. They may know the strengths and weaknesses of the proposed potential candidates.

SCREENING CRITERIA

Once the objectives are set and a list of candidates is compiled, the third step in the acquisition process would be to establish a set of criteria which the potential candidates must meet. These criteria would include but not be limited to the following:

1. Size of the company to be acquired.

2. Type of acquisition.

3. Minimum ROI.

4. Growth potential of the candidate.

5. Capital needs of the candidate: financial or human capital.

6. Market potential and the candidate's current and projected market share.

7. Preliminary financial review of liquidity, activity, and profitability ratios.

SELECTION AND PRELIMINARY DISCUSSION

Having used the screening criteria, the acquirer must be in a position to rank the candidates by using 1, 2, 3, 4, etc. with "1" as the most important candidate based on preliminary financial review. Detailed financial investigation and research should follow. However, the acquirer backed-up with the preliminary financial information must pursue the most highly preferred candidate first. The technique in the initial approach can generate a congenial business environment for a long and pleasant discussion or it can create an atmosphere non-conducive to a continued dialogue. Therefore, the acquirer would be better off following these suggested techniques:

1. A sincere approach telling the candidate's management why you want to see him.

2. An offer to meet with him at their office is recommended. This would assist in giving the acquirer some insight into the candidate's operation.

3. A simplified list of questions that could be readily answered without putting management on the spot.

4. A willingness to give the candidate's management the information they need within reason.

5. A time schedule for a follow-up meeting where additional financial information about the candidate's firm should be available for discussion.

The fact that the acquirer schedules a first visit without a follow-up would keep the candidate's management thinking of what to expect next. This may result in a climate of confusion and bitterness on the part of the candidate's management, even though the acquirer is interested but is not sure of his business schedule for a follow-up meeting.

PRICE DETERMINATION

In the determination of a purchase price, it is imperative that the acquirer utilize two of the following methods for comparative purposes:

1. Book Value - This involves the net worth of a company based on the accounting principle of assets equal liabilities plus capital equity (Assets = Liabilities + Capital Equity).

2. Fair Market Value - This involves the appraisal of physical assets and the current market value of working capital. In utilizing this method, careful

attention must be given to bad debts as well as to the inventory method used.

3. Stock Market Value - The stock price should be analyzed and carefully utilized. Comparative analysis to the stock of other companies in the same line of business is recommended.

4. Price/Earning Ratio (P/E) - The projected earnings per share of the seller should be utilized. However, it should be noted that the market value under this method is determined if the P/E ratio is estimated. The following formula can he used: Market Value of a Share = EPS x P/E Ratio.

5. Present Value of Future Cash Flow - This involves utilizing the future cash flows of the seller over a period of at least ten (10) years (depending on the life of the business) and discounting these cash flows using the acquirer's expected ROI.

APPLICATION OF ACQUISITION PRICING METHODS

Suppose that the acquirer, through his sources, has come to a selection of a candidate for acquisition. The candidate selected is forty-nine percent (49%) owned by the acquirer. The acquirer is interested in obtaining total control of the business and thus is planning on acquiring the additional fifty-one percent (51 %). What method should the acquirer use to determine the purchase price of the additional interest sought?

To clearly illustrate the acquisition price determination methods discussed earlier, let us assume the following:

1. That "M" is the acquiring corporation.

2. That "J" is the candidate being acquired.

3. That M is a multinational corporation.

4. That J used to be a family-owned company before selling forty-nine percent (49%) interest to M.

5. That J's current fifty-one percent (51%) is owned by two brothers who inherited the business from their father.

6. That M is an American-based company while J is a German-based company.

CANDIDATE IDENTIFICATION AND PURCHASE PRICE DETERMINATION

7. That J's total common shares are 701,961 of which 343,961 are currently owned by M.

Since M owns forty-nine percent (49%) of J, M must have all the necessary information needed to make the decision regarding the acquisition. However, the concern here is the illustration of the price determination methods. In determining the purchase price of the fifty-one percent (51 %) interest in J, two methods are considered. These methods are as follows:

1. Present value of future cash flows.

2. Price/earning ratio or multiple.

Present value method - The present value method involves discounting the future cash flows. For this case, 2000 through 2004 projected profit after tax is utilized. Incremental profit after tax resulting from the fifty-one percent (51%) ownership is considered in addition to the increase or decrease in the incremental investment. That is, a more detailed analysis of assets and liabilities is used to determine the cash flow rather than the simplistic approach of profit after tax plus depreciation equal to the cash flow. To simplify the calculation further, fiscal 2004 cash flow for the company J is assumed as annual cash flow continuing through fiscal 2009. The residual value of the fifty-one percent (51 %) acquisition is estimated to be equal to the estimated net worth of J at that time. The calculated price can then be based on discounting the cash flows, the result of which is presented in Table 8.1.

Table 8.1

Estimated Value of "J" Equity

(Millions of Dollars)

Discount Rate	J's Sale Value	Price of * 51% Interest
10.0%	$24.4	$12.4
12.0%	21.9	11.1
15.0%	18.8	9.6

* Figures Rounded to the nearest one hundred thousand

Table 8.1 reflects a purchase price based on cash flows related to the equity of J only. If the total capital employed by J is considered instead of equity only, then the results should he as reflected in Table 8.2.

Table 8.2

Estimated Value of "J" Investment

(Millions of Dollars)

	10 Year Life				Infinite Life			
Discount Rate	Total Value*	Less J's Debt*	Equity Value*	51% of Equity	Total Value*	Less J's Debt	Equity Value*	51% of Equity*
10.0%	$29.0	$(21.2)	$7.8	$4.0	$38.0	$(21.2)	$16.8	$8.6
12.0%	$26.0	$(21.2)	$4.8	$2.5	$32.0	$(21.2)	$10.8	$5.5
15.0%	$23.0	$(21.2)	$1.8	$1.0	$25.0	$(21.2)	$3.8	$2.0

* Figures Rounded to the nearest one hundred thousand.

Price/Earning Multiple Ratio - In determining the price earning ratio, investigation should be made in the stock market for listed companies comparable to "J." However, consultation of Standard and Poor's publication or Dun and Bradstreet Reports is recommended for finding the average P/E multiple. In the case of company "J" located in Germany, it will be essential on the part of corporation M to contact its external auditors (especially if one of the "Big Four" firms) since auditing firms such as Deloitte, Price-Waterhouse-Coopers, Ernst and Young, and KPMG have consulting divisions that are up-to-date on price earnings multiples for similar operations. Suppose that a seven to ten (7-10) multiple of EPS was recommended, then the price should be determined as detailed in Table 8.3.

Table 8.3

J's 51% Estimated Equity Value

P/E Multiple	EPS 5 Yr. $Average	J's Total Est. Value Per Share	51% Of Total Common Stock	Estimated Purchase Price of 51% (Millions)
7	$3.2	$22.4	358000	$8.0
8	3.2	25.6	358000	9.2
9	3.2	28.8	358000	10.3
10	3.2	32.0	358000	11.5

Book Value - In analyzing the book value, the most recent audited balance sheet of "J" must be reviewed. Analysis of working capital should be done. The inventory method utilized by "J" is the same method that is utilized by corporation M, which is the average method. However, J's bad debts are at a minimum since J's major customers are VW and Mercedes Benz as well as other European car manufacturers. A careful review of the aging analysis report shows that the customers are paying on time and that the credit policy as outlined by the J company has been very effective. J's balance sheet for fiscal year (FY) 2000 is as shown in Table 8.4, on the following page.

The approach under this method is to analyze the depreciation methods used, to review the inventories for obsolete material, and to analyze the receivables. Assuming that corporation M would assume the debt and other liabilities as is, then the purchase price for fifty-one percent (51 %) of J is equal to 51 % x Net Worth or 51 % x $13.3 million, which is 6.8 million dollars.

Table 8.4

Corporation J

Consolidated Balance Sheet

FY Ending December 31, 2000

(Millions of Dollars)

ASSETS

Cash	$.4
Marketable Securities	3.1
Receivables (Net of Bad Debts)	10.7
Inventories	<u>20.7</u>
Total Current Assets	$34.9
Fixed Assets (Net of Accum. Dep.)	9.4
Other Assets including Goodwill	<u>.9</u>
TOTAL ASSETS	**$45.2**

LIABILITIES AND CAPITAL EQUITY

Current Liabilities	$14.1
Long-Term Debt	17.8
Equity (Common Stock & Retained Earnings)	<u>13.3</u>
TOTAL LIABILITIES AND CAPTIAL EQUITY	**$45.2**

Fair Market Value - This is achieved by the evaluation of its current assets in terms of the liquidation value of the business and the consequences of a maximum loss to the acquirer. Appraisal of the physical assets including plant and equipment by a professional real estate appraisal and industry expert is part of the market value activity. J's trademarks and business reputation among other competitors must be carefully considered as part of the total fair market value of the firm. Therefore, total market value is equal to the liquidity value of net working capital plus the appraised value of the physical assets, plus goodwill less any long term liability.

Stock Market Value - Should the stock market value be listed in order to determine the price of company J? In the case of J, the company is not listed on the European Exchange or any other exchange and, therefore, a price per share can be determined only on the basis of the stock value of similar corporations. However, where a corporation has a listed stock, then the stock market value can be used and a tender offer can be made to the stockholders to acquire the number of shares needed to achieve the additional fifty-one percent (51 %) ownership.

FINANCING THE ACQUISITION

Analysis of financing methods must be outlined by the acquirer. In this case, corporation M must analyze its acquisition of additional fifty-one percent (51%) interest in company J using the following financing methods:

1. Debt financing.
2. Equity financing.
3. A combination of debt and equity financing.

Under "debt" financing, corporation M would seek funds from lending institutions. Longterm debt should be used and a plan to avoid revolving credit terms is recommended. Revolving lines of credit would be used only if corporation M intends to issue debentures and if debenture approval has been granted by the SEC. The sale of debentures would be used to pay the short-term debt generated by the acquisition. However, financial analysis of the impact of the debt on M's debt ratio as well as on its earnings per share should be analyzed. For example, Table 8.5 explains how debt may impact the EPS if the fifty-one percent (51%) additional acquisition in J is achieved one hundred percent (100%) through debt.

Table 8.5

"M" Additional Profits

FY 2001 – FY 2004

(Millions of Dollars)

	2001	2002	2003	2004
Incremental J Profit After tax resulting from 51% additional ownership	$1.5	$1.4	$1.6	$1.7
11% interest on $8.0 million debt used in the acquisition of J	(.9)	(.9)	(.9)	(.9)
Impact on M's profit After tax (excluding Goodwill)	**$.6**	**$.5**	**$.7**	**$.8**

If the acquisition is financed through the issue of additional common stock, then interest is not a factor and the profit after tax would increase by the interest amount estimated. Nevertheless, the EPS may increase or decrease depending on the additional number of shares issued, but the total debt ratio would improve, thus generating a possible higher credit rating.

Financing through a combination of debt and equity would depend on the ratio of debt to equity. Is it fifty-fifty or thirty-seventy, etc.? This combined strategy would depend on the debt ratio of the corporation and its credit rating, as well as its ability to achieve permission from the SEC for a new issue of shares.

A factor that should be considered in "price determination" is the size of the goodwill. In this case of corporation M, M should have paid 6.8 million dollars for company J (51% of $13.3 million), instead of 8.0 million dollars, which resulted in $1.2 million dollars of goodwill. This goodwill could be recorded under the "purchase method" of accounting and amortized over fifteen (15) year period beginning with the month in which the acquisition is accomplished. FASB must be reviewed relative to impairment of goodwill. However, it should be noted that prior to the introduction of FASB 141, it was possible for corporation M to acquire the additional fifty-one percent (51%) in J and to have no goodwill recorded regardless of the purchase price paid. The "no" goodwill approach used to be available under the "pooling-of-interest" method and is no longer a possibility for the M Corporation to utilize such an accounting method. Therefore, M must use the "purchase" method, and record a goodwill of $1.2 million, which would impact the profit position, since goodwill amortization must be amortized for a 15 year period according to Section 197 of the Internal Revenue Code.[1]

It can be realized from this analysis that the determination of the purchase price can be calculated accurately if an investigation into the accounting records is done and the data used are not jeopardized by future legal actions against the assets presented by the seller. Chapter 9 discusses the negotiation process as well as the procedure used for the verification of the accounting and legal records.

---

1 "Internal Revenue Code: Sec. 197: Amortization of Goodwill and Certain Other Intangibles." Tax Almanac. 31 July 2007 http://www.taxalmanac.org/index.;h;/Sec._197._Amortization_of_goodwill_and_certain_other_intangibles

CHAPTER 9

NEGOTIATION AND INVESTIGATION OF ACCOUNTING AND LEGAL RECORDS

What items should a follow-up meeting by the acquirer consider?

What conditions are important for an acquirer to have a successful response from the seller's management?

What accounting information should be reviewed?

What are some of the items a task force might review in examining a potential acquisition?

What should the legal counsel review in general?

What specific legal considerations must be reviewed?

What other areas of the business, besides accounting and legal, should be reviewed?

What are the characteristics of a good investigation report?

Once an identification of the company to be acquired is made and a purchase price is determined, the initial contact with an intention of meeting the seller at the premises is recommended. A follow-up of the initial contact is important. Representatives of the two corporations will meet and information requested by the acquirer during the first meeting can then be reviewed.

The objectives of the negotiation should be outlined clearly by the acquirer. These objectives would include the acquirer's determination to:

1. Initially get acquainted with the seller's management through a short visit with the intention of testing the attitude of the seller's management toward the acquisition.

2. Obtain additional information that might be essential for continued dialogue.

3. Find out areas of business interest.

4. Explore a purchase price or stock exchange ratio.

5. Anticipate and outline any conversion problem that might result from the acquisition.

CONDITIONS FOR SUCCESSFUL NEGOTIATIONS

Obtaining the exact information that the acquirer needs may remain a problem throughout the acquisition process. Companies sometimes are not sure that they desire to be acquired. Therefore, they may reject any request for certain detailed information about their financial position.

How the acquirer attempts to handle this rejection is an important aspect of the negotiation process. Success of the negotiation, therefore, depends on the cooperation of the seller's management. For the seller's management to cooperate, certain conditions must prevail. These conditions should involve the acquirer's awareness:

1. To keep the negotiation confidential.

2. To avoid bringing legal counsel into the first and second meeting.

3. To set up a timetable that is reasonable for compiling the information needed.

4. To prepare a check list of questions to be answered without duplicating the effort of the seller's management and staff.

INVESTIGATION PROCESS

The investigation team organized by the acquirer's management in consultation with the seller should include two key employees--one representing the acquirer and the other representing the seller. The team should be composed of manufacturing, industrial relations, purchasing, engineering, marketing, accounting, legal and financial personnel.

A coordinator of the team should be appointed. This coordinator must be a key member of the acquirer's management. The coordinator will be responsible for coordinating the investigation activities and setting up the time schedule for the completion of each event. Personnel assignment to different tasks would be the sole responsibility of the coordinator. Once the investigation is completed, it will be the coordinator's responsibility to prepare a report to the acquirer's board of directors. This report should list the pros and cons of the acquisition.

The legal counsel on the team should be responsible for reviewing important documents of the seller while the accountants should verify and check the data supporting the financial information presented by the seller.

Investigation of Accounting Records - The accounting and financial task force should carefully review the seller's records related to the financial information submitted. The review should be designed to cover (1) earnings, (2) unrevealed taxes, (3) inventory methods, (4) depreciation methods, (5) inflated investments, and (6) all liabilities.

If the seller is subject to the SEC regulations, it will be easy for the task force to review financial reports submitted to the SEC. A careful review of these reports should assist the task force in developing historical cost percentages that could be used in reviewing the seller's submitted projections. If the seller's line of business covers more than one product line, it will be essential that the task force analyze the gross profit per product line as well as fixed and semivariable expenses allocated to each product.

Considerations should be given to the way in which generally accepted accounting principles (GAAP) have affected reported profits. Consistency of the GAAP application during the accounting period is important as well as necessary for accurate reporting. If any change in the accounting methods was made, the specific date of change should be noted to assist in evaluating the accounting information presented.

An illustration of the preceding discussion can be exemplified in the careful review of the accounting information presented to General Dynamics by the Chrysler Corporation. The

General Dynamics Corporation acquired the Chrysler Defense Subsidiary in Northeastern Pa. The acquisition took place during 1982 with General Dynamics paying approximately $350 million for the Chrysler Defense Plant. During the month of January, 1982, a task force of the investigation team flew from California to Scranton, Pa., to review the accounting information presented by Chrysler to General Dynamics. The concerns of the task force were as follows:

1. The accuracy of the size of the inventory.

2. The exact balance of receivables.

3. The earnings projected as compared to historical figures.

4. The pension plan.

5. The investment tax credits taken.

6. The amortization of small tools.

7. The capital expenditure expected to meet projected sales as compared to previous sales expenditure ratio.

8. The review of fixed assets belonging to the U.S. Government versus that of Chrysler.

9. The hidden liabilities that General Dynamics would have to assume.

After careful review of historical and current figures, adjustments to projected earning were made by General Dynamics prior to the consummation of the acquisition.

In addition to ascertaining that all the preceding factors are important in the review process, it is necessary that adequate analysis of the bad debt provisions be made. Actual bad debt can exceed provisions in certain cases. Accounting and financial concern should be a factor in reviewing the seller's return and warranty policies. Return and allowances provided by the seller could be underestimated which may lead the acquirer into future unforeseen financial liabilities.

The financial statement reflecting the current status must he audited carefully, regardless of whether the seller is subject to the SEC regulations or is a family-owned company.

The evaluation of the equipment and physical plant is a matter of judgment. While the depreciation methods used may be accepted, the salvage value of the equipment may not.

Therefore, a look at the utilization of life versus equipment obsolescence must be considered by the manufacturing task force, not the accountants.

The liability side of the balance sheet should involve an audit for unrecorded debt. The auditing method in such a situation would depend on the skill of the task force. For example, a skillful auditor can verify the accounts payable figures on the balance sheet by referencing the receiving reports, the invoices, and the payments made subsequent to the balance sheet date. This can be further achieved by taking the beginning balance, adding all payables and subtracting disbursements related to invoices.

Accrued liabilities can often be detected by a knowledge of the line of business. For example, ingenuity on the part of the task force can generally determine hidden aspects in these accounts.

Questions such as, What can be accrued? Is it accrued payroll, payroll taxes, FICA, vacation, holiday pay, etc. could be raised. The task force should review lease obligations in line with the Financial Accounting Standard Board (FASB) number thirteen (13). Lease terminations and subsequent financial obligations must be considered in terms of the financial impact on earnings. The investigation of the liability side should involve a careful review of sales contracts. Has the seller received any customer advances on any contract? Or has the customer advanced any cash to the seller which was not reflected under sales?

Although financial records are important to the task force, the legal review remains as important as the financial review since legal findings of pending cases may result in a financial liability to the acquirer.

Investigation of Legal Records - The legal counsel assigned to the acquisition must review the following:

1. Seller's corporate charter and articles of incorporation.

2. Minutes of all executive committee meetings.

3. Minutes of the board of directors meetings.

4. Minutes of shareholders meetings.

5. Activities of the corporation under acquisition and all its subsidiaries, domestic and international.

As a matter of this initial review, the legal counsel may he enlightened as to any pending lawsuit against the seller. Therefore, further investigation by the legal counsel should identify violations (if any) of Anti-Trust Laws. This should include any past and future violations by the seller. If no violation is found, then the counsel should concentrate on the legal considerations surrounding the acquisition. These considerations would include:

1. Labor contract agreement between the seller and its respective union.

2. State laws in which the seller is incorporated and operating. This involves the analysis of state requirements regarding the retention of the seller's assets in the state to satisfy the seller's creditors.

3. The impact of the type of transaction on the legal success of the acquisition.

4. The violation of Section Seven (7) of the Clayton Act or any federal law such as the Sherman Act regarding conspiracy and monopoly, the FTC regarding unfair competition and Robinson Patman Act regarding price discrimination.

5. The timing of the public announcement and the SEC regulations.

6. The legal requirement regarding acquirer's shareholders approval and the timing of the transaction approval by seller's shareholders.

In addition to the accounting and legal investigations, there should be a thorough investigation of the business. The business investigation should involve areas such as marketing, manufacturing, engineering and industrial relations.

Investigation of General Business - The acquirer's team should review the seller's total market potential as well as the seller's pricing methods. Seller's channels of distribution and sales mix should he analyzed and comments by the respective team members be made, if necessary. Members of the team should be assigned to study the seller's sales organization in order to determine whether future projected sales could be achieved. Review of the sales methods employed, the salesmen compensation, the zone district office locations, as well as the sales policies involving discounts, returns and allowances should be made.

While part of the team analyzes the seller's marketing strategy, the advertising programs, and the sales policies, other members should concentrate on reviewing the current personnel status of the seller. This investigation should involve (1) the adequacy of office staff and line management, (2) compensation method used, (3) employment contracts extension, (4) working conditions and physical arrangements of offices, (5) personnel policies regarding profit sharing and health insurance, and (6) employee morale and quality of life work.

Further investigation by team members should include the production and procurement methods used. This involves (a) product lines and production facilities, (b) engineering personnel, (c) research and development, (d) quality control and inspection methods used, (e) production efficiency, (f) patents and trademarks held, and (g) storage and warehousing facilities provided.

Although these are most of the items that should he investigated by the acquirer's teams, nevertheless they should not be considered a complete investigation list but one that could be used as an initial start in an investigation process.

Investigation Report - Once the members of the team have completed their investigation, the coordinator should submit a summary report to the acquirer's management and through them to the board of directors. It is imperative that the findings be expressed in writing. The characteristics of the report should be as follows:

1. Concise and clear report.

2. Presentation of the facts and not a flickering recitation of the investigation procedure.

3. Integration of the finding of several members of the team.

4. Outline of the problems and important business topics that should be considered/resolved prior to the consummation of the acquisition.

While the negotiation and investigation can resolve some of the problems that may arise, there can be other considerations that the acquirer must not overlook. These considerations may involve the acquisition of overseas and family-owned firms, which is the subject of Chapter 10.

CHAPTER 10

ACQUISITION CONSIDERATIONS OF OVERSEAS COMPANIES

What major items should be considered in an overseas acquisition?

What is a joint venture and when is it used?

What restrictions may a country place on foreign ownership of its companies?

What is the effect of currency exchange risk on acquisition of an overseas company?

As stated in Chapter 9, there are major items to be considered in an overseas acquisition before negotiations commence between the acquirer and the seller. Therefore, it is the acquirer's responsibility to review key factors prior to the initial contact. Some of these key factors involve the country in which the potential seller is located and are as follows:

1. Political stability.
2. Currency stability.
3. Inflation rate.
4. Import restrictions.
5. Restrictions on repatriation of profits.
6. Capital requirement by the acquirer.
7. Maximum percentage of ownership that can be achieved by the acquirer.
8. Tax Laws.
9. Government intervention in business.

After careful analysis of the risk factors outlined, the acquirer should make the decision on whether to pursue this acquisition further. If the decision is positive, then financial analysis should follow. However, the acquirer's analytical work must reflect the tax impact of capitalized retained earning and the consequences of possible future political instability of the country in which the potential candidate is located. Foreign anti-trust laws must be considered in the analysis process.

ANTI-TRUST LAWS AND STATUTORY REGULATIONS OF FOREIGN COUNTRIES

Most foreign anti-trust laws concern themselves with fair trade practices. For example, Germany's "cartel law" aims at preventing a buildup of economic power wherever it restricts competition and adversely affects the maximum supply of goods and services. In addition, acquisition of corporations or family-owned businesses must be reported to the appropriate authority in situations where the business combination would result in unfair competition of a specific market. However, the Federal Cartel Office is working closely with the European Economic Commission and therefore the Maastricht Treaty is currently playing a role in the approval or disapproval of acquisitions or divestments.

If the acquirer, as a U.S. Corporation, intends to acquire a firm in any country of the European Economic Community (EEC) or European Union (EU), then the acquirer's legal counsel should carefully review the Treaty Establishing the European Community (TEEC) which superceeded the Treaty of Rome, prior to pursuing the acquisition negotiation. This TEEC is the one by which the EEC was established. Articles eighty one (81), eighty-five (85), and eighty-six (86) of the treaty provide information regarding competition, price-fixing, market sharing and unfair monopoly while Article 54 covers acquisition of land and building and the set up of branches or subsidiaries. The financial reporting, capital maintenance, corporate acquisitions, as well as public disclosure are all part of the TEEC articles fifty-four through one hundred sixteeen (54-116), and must be reviewed by coporations seeking acquisitions of companies in the EU.[1]

FOREIGN COUNTRY RESTRICTIONS

Acquirers may have to concern themselves with the ownership factor. This case may cause an acquisition to shift from a merger transaction to that of a joint venture. The joint venture most often develops in countries where governmental restrictions hinder the acquirer from becoming a major holder in the firm being acquired. Therefore, an association between the acquirer on the one hand and the local owners on the other is then established. Such an established association is termed a joint venture. Local owners can be the host government itself or any other ongoing publicly held company.

The approach to a joint venture may assist the acquirer in reducing political risk through national interference of local executives with their own governments. In a few foreign countries, red tape plays a major aspect in the acquisition process. Although this may be low key in developed countries, it can be a major factor in developing countries as well as the less developed ones.

In the case of wealthy oil rich countries, percentage of ownership by a local national may be specified by the government, which puts the acquirer at a disadvantage for major ownership. For example, in Saudi-Arabia the percentage of ownership for a non-Saudi is restricted to a forty percent (40%) participation in the oil industry and banking services. However, a minimum of twenty-five percent (25%) is required ownership by Saudi in other business sectors. Furthermore, it should be emphasized that all foreign capital investment in Saudi-Arabia is regulated and controlled by the "Foreign Capital Investment Office" of the Ministry of Commerce and Industry. Any foreign capital involvement must be licensed, which means that a thorough review by the "Foreign Capital Investment Committee" must take place and the investor must comply with a prescribed investment schedule. This investment schedule must be followed or the investment project may be in jeopardy.

---

1 "Treaty Establishing the European Community." Hellenic Resources Network. 2007. 27 July 2007 http://www.hri.org/docs/Rome57/index.html

Other restrictions may deal with imports of goods or sub-parts to the local country of the candidate under study. For example, although there is no restriction on foreign ownership in Sweden (except in mines, forests and land), prior approval by the Swedish exchange control authorities is required of imports. Therefore, licenses should be on hand prior to importing any product from other countries. In some cases, this can impact the output of a manufacturing or assembly plant where certain elements of raw material must be imported in order to complete the product in the host country. Careful analysis of the seller's sales projections in light of import accessibility must be done as part of the evaluation process.

Restrictions by a country can really impact the ROI. For example, restriction of dividends to the United States from certain host countries can be heavily taxed when the dividend is in excess of a specified percentage of the profit achieved by the subsidiary. So the financial analyst must weigh the tax burden of repatriation of profit versus the risk of capitalized retained earnings.

However, capitalization of retained earnings and overseas subsidiary growth achieved in a foreign country may he a risky decision. Therefore, the question of restriction versus the future value of the sale of the company must take into consideration the inflation rate of the country as well as the future value of its currency. Therefore, currency exchange is very important in an overseas acquisition attempt.

CURRENCY EXCHANGE

The progressive acquirer must look at the currency exchange risk. This is particularly true in a pre-planned acquisition for major control of overseas companies. FASB number nine (9) must be utilized in establishing the basis for translating the financial statement as well as the projected data. These translated data would in time be used to determine the EPS impact of the acquisition on the acquirer's financial position.

There are several points that must be considered when trying to acquire an overseas company. However, nationalism and national interest of the overseas contact must not be ignored. Furthermore, the market entry restrictions and the foreign government aids in terms of tax concessions and investment guarantees should be weighed in the analysis process. Once this aspect of the investigation is completed, the price is determined, and the verbal agreement is reached; then an acquisition contract must be drafted. How this acquisition contract should be structured is the subject of the next chapter.

CHAPTER 11

ACQUISITION CONTRACT AND THE CLOSING PROCESS

What is included in a seller's memorandum of intent?

What questions should an attorney consider in drawing up the acquisition contract?

What are the two functions of the acquisition contract?

What does an acquisition contract include?

The acquisition contract should come after the investigation is completed and the price is determined by the acquirer. However, prior to the investigation the acquirer and the seller may have certain concerns that might impact the acquisition. For example, although an agreement in principle may have been established between the acquirer and the seller, the acquirer may still be concerned about the seller's negotiation with a third party during the investigation process. Also, a concern of the seller may be the buyer's intent to consummate the acquisition if all the facts presented in the verbal agreement were confirmed by the investigation team.

The seller's concern may he reduced through a memorandum of intent which would outline the general terms of the acquisition including a narrative of the business to be acquired, the type of transaction through which the acquisition would be achieved, the SEC related procedure, the IRS rulings, a commitment by the acquirer to submit a copy of the investigation team report to the seller, and conditions requiring the acquirer to keep the investigation confidential. This memorandum of intent would be signed by both the acquirer and the seller. During the investigation, the legal counsel working with the investigation team through the team coordinator should draft the acquisition contract.

FACTORS IMPACTING THE CONTRACT

The development of the "acquisition contract" should be based on the coordination of efforts between the investigation team on the one side and the legal counsel of the acquirer on the other side. A clear line of communication should be established by the lawyer (legal counsel) with the accounting and financial task force. Also the legality of marketing certain products as well as impacting the environment makes it necessary for the other members of the team, such as the manufacturing and marketing personnel, to converse with the lawyer drafting the detailed contract. In addition, labor laws and the union contracts force the lawyer to clearly review the labor agreement and confer with the industrial relations task force. Therefore, the focal point of communication, during the investigation process, should be the lawyer's office since the lawyer has the basic responsibility for preparing the detailed acquisition contract.

Before a detailed contract is drafted, the lawyer must establish a check list to answer questions that are of help in completing the contract. This check list, if properly structured, would clarify several communication barriers between the attorney (lawyer) and the investigation team. Some of the questions that the attorney must answer, through the team coordinator, are as follows:

1. Is the stock or the asset being acquired?

2. How will the payment be made to the seller? Will it be in cash or in stock?

3. Is the transaction a taxable or a tax-free one?

4. Is the transaction a plan of reorganization and merger? Or is it a stock purchase transaction?

5. In what state was the seller incorporated?

6. Is the seller under bankruptcy proceedings under Chapter XI of the Bankruptcy Act?

As these questions are answered, the attorney is then in the process of asking additional questions regarding tax deficiencies for past years and other types of liability. The communication link between the attorney and the investigation team should be paralleled by the communication link between the attorney and the acquirer's executives as well as the acquirer's auditors. As the contract is developed, it should be the attorney's responsibility to convey pertinent information on various liability aspects of the acquisition to the respective executives of the acquirer.

ACQUISITION CONTRACT

Two functions are achieved through a well drawn-up contract. These functions are:

1. The legal rights of the acquirer and the seller as well as their obligations to one another regarding the acquisition transaction become fixed through execution of the contract.

2. The information on the seller's business and the liability of the acquirer resulting from the acquisition is documented and becomes clear to the acquirer.

To achieve these functions, the acquisition contract must therefore follow an organized pattern. This organized pattern includes, but is not limited to, the following:

1. General statement of agreement between the acquirer and the seller should include:

    a. Identification of their state of incorporation.

    b. Expression of any plan of reorganization.

    c. Identification of the section of the IRS Code under which such plan may be adopted.

2. General Terms of the acquisition

   a. Effective date of the acquisition or merger.

   b. Manner and basis of payment.

   c. Manner and basis of converting the shares and the terms of conversion, if any.

   d. Election of cash exchange, if relevant.

   e. Shares to be transferred under the plan of reorganization, if applicable.

   f. Shares to be transferred in escrow, if applicable.

3. Assets to be acquired by the acquirer.

4. Acquirer's assumptions of seller's liabilities.

5. Representations and warranties of the seller.

   a. Organization and good standing of the seller in the state of incorporation.

   b. Operations outside the state of incorporation and relationship to acquisition.

   c. Specifications of authorized and issued capital stock.

   d. Financial statement prepared in accordance with general accepted accounting principles reflecting all necessary adjustments for a fair presentation of the operating results.

      (1) balance sheet with specification of any irregularities (i.e.) inventory shortage or obsolescence.
      (2) earning statement presenting accurately the results of operation.

   e. Undisclosed liabilities including any prior years of federal, state or local tax liability not reflected on the balance sheet.

   f. Statement expressing that neither the seller nor any of its officers is engaged or threatened with any legal action.

6. Representations and warranties of the acquirer.

    a. Acquirer's organizational structure.

    b. Acquirer's capitalization and stock status.

    c. Acquirer's financial position.

    d. Other facts regarding the acquirer and its management.

7. Specification of payment of finders fees, if any; conduct of the seller's and buyer's business pending closing.

8. Conditions of the conduct of business by the seller following closing.

9. Time schedule of delivery of inventions, employment contract, keys, etc. of the seller to the acquirer.

10. General provisions covering all other items not specified in items one through nine which would include content of employment contract, employees' benefits, stock option plan, executive contracts, anti-trust escape statements, etc.

In addition to all the items mentioned, the acquisition contract must be supplemented with exhibits reflecting the financial position of the seller as well as the seller's lease agreements, along with a list of major suppliers and stockholders.

CLOSING PROCESS

Once the acquisition contract is written, it should be reviewed by both the seller's and the acquirer's legal counsel. If approval is granted by both legal counsels, then the signing and delivery of contract should take place. The activity of execution of the contract by both the acquirer and the seller fixes the time of the consummation of the acquisition. If the acquisition is a "stock acquisition," the title to the seller's stock is then transferred to the acquirer via the endorsement of the stock certificates. However, if the acquisition is an "asset acquisition," title to the seller's assets is transferred to the acquirer through the proper bill of sale or any other related document.

PART FOUR

Divestment Procedure

CHAPTER 12

DIVESTMENT VERSUS RETENTION: CANDIDATE RECOGNITION

What should a divestment plan of action include?

What should the preliminary financial evaluation of a potential candidate for divestment consider?

What financial ratios are helpful in evaluating the candidate for divestment?

How should these ratios be tabulated?

It is essential that the defined objectives of divestment be stated and a prompt evaluation of the ailing subsidiaries and divisions be done. Study of various alternatives should be a managerial goal prior to any public announcement of the intention to divest.

The disposition of partial assets or total on-going operations must be the result of a well structured plan of action. This plan of action must include:

1. A well-organized procedure for evaluating an on-going operation and identifying candidates for divestment.

2. A devised system for relating the objectives of divestment to the selected candidates.

3. A developed approach for reviewing certain aspects of the operation with the intention of retention.

4. A time frame and a program evaluation review technique (PERT) through which the intended divestment should be accomplished.

5. A managerial prospective of reinvestment opportunities and the opportunity cost factors impacting the parent company.

Once this plan is designed, then the process of implementation should follow. The first approach would be a general financial review of each operation.

PRELIMINARY FINANCIAL EVALUATION

In order to be able to recognize potential candidates for divestment, the parent company must review each of its operations. The review should consider:

1. The background of the operation, which involves:

    a. The origination of the subsidiary or division.

    b. The current status of the operation.

    c. The process which leads to the manufacturing of the current products or to the current services being offered.

2. A ten-year financial summary reflecting five years of historical data and five years of projected data. This summary should include the sales, profit before and after tax and the return on assets.

3. A careful analysis of the subsidiary or division's fixed assets.

4. An analysis of the operation's product lines with a summary write-up of each product line and a financial review of the past five years as well as the future projection for a five-year period. The data for the product line analysis should include sales, gross profit, net profit before and after tax (with allocated fixed cost), and a return on assets (ROA) based on an estimated asset base per product line.

5. A concluding paragraph commenting on whether the financial performance of the operation over the period analyzed has been satisfactory or unsatisfactory and the impact it had made on the corporate EPS.

Once this preliminary evaluation is done, the logical candidates for divestment can be sorted out. However, there may exist more than one candidate which would lead management to the decision as to which should be divested first.

IDENTIFICATION OF KEY FINANCIAL FACTORS

Based on the actual and projected financial data, the candidates can be further evaluated by analyzing their cash flow position. This would involve the capital expenditure needed to achieve the projected sales and profits as well as the cost of capital. The cost of capital would be utilized to determine the present value (PV) of future projected cash flows (CF) from the operation under study. Therefore, calculation of the book value of the assets based on the current balance sheet should be used to determine the internal rate of return (IRR), or as it is commonly referred to, the discounted cash flow (DCF) rate. Projection should then extend beyond five years, as the fifth year cash flow can be used for an additional five years, unless the operation is expected to retrogress due to technological change.

The DCF calculation is expected to determine the yield on the investment. It differs from the net present value (NPV) in that it does not reflect the size of the investment. For example, two operations may have the same DCF rate but yet a different investment base. The net present value takes into consideration the present value of the cash flow at the cost of capital or opportunity cost and the investment base (NPV = PV of CF minus Investment). However, the NPV for the two operations may be different despite the fact that the DCF rate is the same.

Calculation of the ROA should be part of the evaluation. Although the ROA is a profitability ratio, it should be based on an activity ratio, which is the asset turnover (ATO), determined by dividing sales by total assets

$$\left(ATO = \frac{Sales}{Total\ Assets} \right)$$

In addition, the return on sales, profitability ratio should be part of the ROA calculation.

The ROS is a key financial indicator in the historical as well as the projected performance of any operation. This ROS is determined by dividing the net income after tax from an operation by the sales of that operation

$$\left(ROS = \frac{Net\ Income\ After\ Tax}{Sales} \right)$$

In calculating the ROA for each operation, the analyst must remember that the ROA is important and any of the following formulas could be used. However, formula number three (3) is preferable.

1. $ROA = \dfrac{Net\ Income\ After\ Tax}{Sales} \times \dfrac{Sales}{Total\ Assets}$

2. $ROA = \dfrac{Net\ Income\ After\ Tax}{Sales}$

3. $ROA = ROS \times ATO$

Formula number three (3) is the same as formula number one (1); however, since in the ranking process of the investment candidates the ROS, ATO and ROA are used, it is recommended that the calculation of the ROA be made after the ROS and ATO are calculated.

The leverage ratio of each operation must be analyzed. The analysis must be concentrated on the debt ratio (DR). The DR is calculated by dividing total debt by total assets (DR = Total Debt/Total Assets). The analysis of the DR should be compared with that of the average industry. In addition, the DR for the parent company should be calculated with and without the divestiture under evaluation. The difference between the percentage points should be figured out in the analysis as part of the liquidation factors essential in the decision-making process.

The impact of the operation on the EPS should play a great role in the identification procedure. The EPS impact on the parent company should be studied. An analysis including calculation of the EPS with and without each operation in question should be done.

RANKING OF POTENTIAL DIVESTMENT CANDIDATES

The individual rates and ratios discussed for each operation, once calculated, should be tabulated. The tabulation of these ratios should be done in a format covering (1) the historical financial picture, (2) the current liquidity position of the operation, and (3) the financial projection of the operation in the future.

Since a review of a ten-year financial summary reflecting a five-year history and a fiveyear projection was recommended earlier, it is, therefore, important that the individual ratios be summarized under three categories for a five-year period. The design of the tabulation should be in a matrix format which is illustrated in Table 12.1.

**Table 12.1
Corporation X (Parent Co.)
Divestment Ranking Analysis**

Intended Year of Divestment	Subsidiary or Division	Historical Ratios (2001 – 2005) ATO*	ROS*	ROA*	Performance to Plan	Present Financial Status CR*	Change in DR*	Future Projections (2006 – 2010) ATO	ROS	IRR/DCF*	Ranking Total
1	A	13	6	8	1	2	2	20	3	10	65
	B	5	8	4	4	1	-2	7	5	8	40
	C	10	8	8	5	3	4	10	6	12	66
2	D	3	-7	-2	2	1	-1	5	8	8	17
	E	6	5	3	4	2	1	7	6	10	44
	F	10	5	5	3	2	2	15	10	15	67

* Explanation of Acronyms : ATO = Asset Turn Over; ROS = Return On Sales; ROA = Return On Assets; CR = Current Ratio; DR = Debt Ratio; IRR = Internal Rate of Return

The matrix would reflect the intended year of divestment, the operation's name, the historical sketch reflecting an average five-year ratio, as well as the ranking of the operation compared to other operations relative to the achievement of the financial plan. This ranking of achieving the plan would be identified by 1, 2, 3, 4, 5, with five (5) reflecting plan achievement, four (4) slightly off by less than ten percent (10%), three (3) off by more than ten percent (10%) but less than thirty percent (30%) two (2) off by more than 30 percent (30%) but less than fifty percent (50%) and one (1) off by more than fifty percent (50%).

The current liquidation and leverage factors would include the current ratio of the operation under study. This current ratio would reflect the present financial status of the operation, while the debt ratio would reflect the percentage points of change in the parent company with and without the operation under evaluation. If the parent company's debt ratio would increase without the operation, then the percentage point of change would be shown as negative on the matrix. If the total debt ratio decreases, the percentage point of change is then reflected as a positive figure.

The future projection category in the matrix would reflect an average five-year ratio with the IRR or DCF rate reflected, based on the present book value of the investment and the future cash flows generated, with a residual value of the investment at the end of the fifth year. The total column reflecting the sum of the factors presented would be used as the ranking column. The operations with the lowest total would be placed first on the divestment schedule and vice versa.

Once the ranking is completed, the parent corporation must decide whether the division or subsidiary should be divested or retained. Therefore, financial analysis and evaluation of different alternatives must be done by management. The process which management should follow to arrive at the final decision is the subject of Chapter 13.

CHAPTER 13

FINANCIAL COMPARISON OF RETENTION, DIVESTMENT, AND REINVESTMENT ALTERNATIVES

What are some of the factors to consider for retention of a candidate previously selected for divestment?

In what ways can divestment take place? What four specific methods can assist in implementing divestment?

What items should be reviewed for the sale of stock method?

What items should he reviewed for the liquidation method?

How do reinvestment opportunities affect divestment?

The evaluation of the operation under divestment consideration should focus primarily on the financial analysis as stated in Chapters 6 and 12. A summary report including the following should be prepared:

1. Brief historic sketch.
2. Market information.
3. Technological position.
4. Manufacturing capabilities.

Although the above items are part of the recognition process, it is important that further analysis be made to satisfy corporate objectives and determine the operation's impact on the corporate consolidated bottom line.

If the subsidiary or division according to the summary report review shows poor performance and ranks the lowest in the "divestment ranking analysis," then a decision must follow. If the management decision is to divest, management must formulate a corresponding decision of reinvestment. The decision to reinvest must be pursued in the light of the alternative to improve and retain the operation. Therefore, "retention" should be viewed as a viable alternative by management and the time and effort should be expended in analyzing the benefits that would be found in retention.

RETENTION ANALYSIS

Several factors should he examined to determine if retention is financially feasible. These factors include the following:

1. Capital requirement.
2. Capital expenditure and the impact on increased revenue.
3. Time involved in rehabilitation of the operation under study.
4. Cost factors associated with automation, reorganization, and renovation of the operation.
5. Government obligations.
6. Impact of government programs on the operation, i.e., programs that allow for tax benefits, investment grants, etc.

FINANCIAL COMPARISON OF RETENTION, DIVESTMENT, AND REINVESTMENT ALTERNATIVES

7. Parent company requirement for debt guarantees.

8. Labor union contract that may be renegotiated to reduce labor cost and avoid possible complications in the divestment.

9. Relation of the operation to the overall corporation, i.e., sale of one operation may have a dramatic effect on another division or subsidiary's cost and sales.

10. Future impact of competition on the operation's market share. For example, increase in total market share as a result of future government programs. Also improvement of market share as a result of the decrease in future competition.

11. Impact of licensing and marketing programs of the operation on the overall sales of the corporation.

Careful review of the items stated should be compared to the divestment proposal. The financial impact on the parent corporation should be analyzed. The determination of the retention plan requires management to assign a study team to evaluate this alternative and arrive at a conclusion. Sales estimates based on additional capital expenditure must be part of the recalculation of the IRR/DCF rate of return of the retention. Also the determination of the contribution that the additional capital expenditure would make to the operation and the operation's respective contribution to the EPS, if the retention plan was adopted, must be made.

DIVESTMENT ANALYSIS

Divestment can take place either by (1) selling the operation as a going concern or by (2) liquidating the assets and paying the liabilities, thereby ending the operation's existence. The financial analyst should calculate the impact of each divestment alternative on the parent corporation. The optional financial divestment alternative would be the one that provides the parent company with the highest amount of net cash flow from operation or its equivalent upon calculating the present value of the cash flow.

Analysis of divestment should cover the overall operation. The financial analyst assigned to do such a task must communicate clearly with accounting, management, research and development, marketing, industrial relations, and the legal department within the corporation. A memorandum from the president or vice-president of the parent company to the president or general manager of a subsidiary or a division should be released, as a first step, explaining in general terms the task of the financial analyst appointed and asking local management to cooperate with the respective person assigned.

The financial analyst, therefore, must make a list of the divestment alternatives. These could include:

1. Sale of stock.

2. Liquidation.

3. Shut down and mothball operation.

4. Divest by issuing subsidiary stock to other stockholders of the parent corporation.

Estimating the cash to he recovered from the divestment may not be an easy task. If the sale of stock is chosen, then the following must be on the analyst's list for calculation:

1. Sale value method of determination.

   a. current value of net worth.

   b. net present value of future earnings.

   c. price/earnings ratio.

2. Original investment base, i.e., tax base.

3. Value of goodwill.

4. Tax benefits from the sale, i.e., capital loss versus capital gain U.S. tax rate.

5. Net effect of the hook value of the loss or gain on the FPS.

6. Estimated cash flow.

7. Estimated debt reduction.

The above should only be analyzed for the sale of stock alternative. If management raises the question, "What about the liquidation impact?," the financial analyst should then be prepared to defend either of the alternatives presented. In the liquidation analysis, the financial analyst should review the following:

1. Cash flow.

FINANCIAL COMPARISON OF RETENTION, DIVESTMENT, AND REINVESTMENT ALTERNATIVES

   a. Net cash flow.

   b. Net cash flow including debt reduction.

2. Liquidation non-recurring costs.

   a. Separation cost.

      (1) severance pay.

      (2) accrued vacations.

      (3) labor contracts.

      (4) county law regarding employee mass termination.

   b. Other closing costs.

      (1) administrative costs - legal costs.

      (2) dismantling and repair cost.

      (3) relocation of supervisory and managerial personnel.

      (4) cancellation of outstanding purchase orders.

      (5) cancellation of outstanding sales contracts.

   c. Cost of lease termination.

      (1) building - if leased.

      (2) equipment, i.e., computer and communication equipment.

      (3) other leases - if any.

3. Tax savings calculations.

   a. Original investment

   b. Incremental investment.

   c. Tax rate applied based on percentage of ownership, i.e., in a liquidation of a subsidiary if the parent company owns eighty percent (80%) or more of the voting stock, then Section 332 of the IRC, applies whereby the subsidiary must distribute all its property in complete redemption of its stock within the taxable year or within three years from the close of the tax year.

   d. Tax-free transaction versus taxable transaction--a review of Sections 331, 332, 333, 334, 337, and 341 of the IRC. Detailed analysis of these sections is shown in Chapter 14 and Appendix A of this book.

4. Valuation of assets.

   a. Warranty may affect receivables and, therefore, one must analyze the bad debt cost due to warranty.
   b. Estimated inventory recovery may vary considerably from book value, depending on the inventory method used, i.e., LIFO or FIFO.
   c. Market value of fixed assets may vary from book value.

      (1) land value may be in excess of book value due to inflation rates since time of the acquisition.
      (2) cost of building may be in excess of book value due to inflation and conditional suitability for other operations.

5. Impact on EPS due to liquidation.

After careful analysis of the various divestment alternatives, the decision to sell, liquidate or mothball the operation may be subject to other considerations. Some of the considerations that may hinder the divestment or make such a plan of action impossible have been outlined in the retention analysis section of this chapter. They may include government requirement, creditors objection, labor contract, etc.

REINVESTMENT OPPORTUNITIES

"Divestitures constitute sound, responsible business management and, in all instances can and should be undertaken for the benefit of the corporation," says Peter Hilton.[1] The benefits, in fact, must be weighed in terms of the financial results of such a divestiture. Reviewing opportunities that will meet the company's standards and goals is an important aspect of managerial tasks. Management, therefore, must set up a target ROI that it expects certain subsidiaries and divisions to meet. If the corporation has other opportunities available which can provide higher returns, then management must pursue those opportunities or otherwise suffer the risk of incurring an opportunity cost to the corporation.

Reinvestment opportunities can be internal and external to the organization. The internal opportunities may involve reduction of current debt which has been borrowed at high interest rates. This will no doubt reduce or eliminate high interest payments.

The external opportunities would be to find an acquisition that will meet the parent company's objectives and which will utilize the investment to its fullest, thus generating an ROI higher than that maintained by the operation under divestment study.

Another reinvestment approach would be the redeployment of assets. Redeployment of assets involves beefing-up operations with higher profits at the expense of thinning those that are less profitable. R. H. Hillman discusses this topic in detail[2]. However, it is important to note that some U.S. corporations have been following this reinvestment approach in recession periods.

COMPARATIVE ANALYSIS OF ALTERNATIVES

The decision to divest any segment of a business has a consequent effect on the parent company. Therefore, in order to keep the profit picture healthy and attractive to investors, management must become concerned with the contribution of each operation within the organization. However, the decision to retain, divest or reinvest becomes simple once all the facts and the assumptions are outlined and included in the financial analysis. The best alternative would be the one that provides the greatest financial gain in terms of profits, costs, cash flows, and ROI. This comparative analysis should assist management in making rational decisions, given the fact that investment opportunities have been identified and analyzed. Furthermore, the simplicity of the decision-making process depends on the accuracy of the

---

1   Peter Hilton, "Divestiture: The Strategic Move on the Corporate Chessboard," *Management Review*, March 1972, p. 16

2   R. H. Hillman, "How to Redeploy Assets," *Harvard Business Review*, November-December, 1971, pp. 95-103.

predicted assumptions utilized in projecting the future events impacting the operation under study.

Although this chapter has focused on the different alternatives involved in the analytical process, it, nevertheless, did not cover the tax implications of divesting domestic and international operations. The different sections of the IRC impacting divestment will be covered in Chapter 14, while an application of the liquidation process of an operation will be discussed in Chapter 15 of this text.

CHAPTER 14

TAX IMPLICATIONS AND CONSIDERATIONS IN DOMESTIC AND INTERNATIONAL DIVESTMENT

What sections of the Internal Revenue Code are applicable to divestment?

What are the important sections relating to the treatment of a gain or a loss to stockholders?

What are some of the tax considerations applicable to divestment?

The tax impact, as stated in Chapter 2, is important in the analysis process of a divestment. Its importance may dictate the method of implementing a divestment decision. Therefore, management must realize this aspect and determine at what stage of the decision it should enter the analysis.

Since divestment involves a gain or loss on disposition, the question of whether the gain or loss is ordinary income or capital gain should be answered. Therefore, the timing of the divestment becomes a factor that management should consider. The decision to retain the operation for an additional year and then divest depends on the company's tax status, as well as the tax treatment of the transaction under evaluation.

The tax treatment in each case determines the direction a corporation follows in divesting. To sell outright, liquidate, retain, or relinquish may be a decision impacted by a section of the Internal Revenue Code.

CODE REQUIREMENTS

The analysis of the IRC as it relates to divestment is very essential in the financial analysis of the divestment. Sections of the code can make a transaction favorable to the parent company while other sections, if misinterpreted, can place corporate management in a groundless position. Therefore, definition of the term "divestment" and interpretation of the relative section of the code are intrinsic factors in the success of the financial analysis. To illustrate the discussion, Sections (Sec.) 332 and 334 of the code will be discussed. These sections, with the related paragraphs, are shown in Appendix A.

Section 332. The conditions of Sec. 332 dictate that no gain or loss shall be recognized on the receipt by corporation X of property allotted in complete liquidation of company Y provided (a) X owns a specified amount of Y's stock, (b) Y's stock is redeemed, and (c) the transfer of Y's property takes place within a specified period of time.

The fact that the term "complete liquidation" is used in the section becomes very important for the analyst to interpret. Therefore, the analyst should further read the regulations to arrive at the definition of the term. For example, the regulations under Sec. 332, if further investigated, would show that the term "complete liquidation" exists when corporation Y ceases to operate and its continued activities are strictly intended for winding up the business, paying the creditors and distributing the remaining cash to the stockholders. Furthermore, to analyze the basis for property in complete liquidation, for property in complete liquidation, the analyst must review Sec. 334.

Section 334. This section specifies that the basis for a property received by the parent company in a liquidation is the fair market value at the time of the liquidation. The analyst must be aware of the content of this section since, in some situations, a parent corporation may want to complete the liquidation of a subsidiary within the framework of Sec. 332 and is unable to dispose of some of the fixed assets within a three (3) year period from "the close of the taxable year during which is made the first of the series of distributions under the plan."[1] By reviewing Sec. 334, the parent company may be able to achieve its tax objective by transferring fixed assets at fair market value, thus consummating the liquidation process within the allowable time frame.

GENERAL CONSIDERATIONS

It is important to know that the liquidation may not only be guided by Sections 332 and 334 but its complexity may involve other sections of the code. Such sections may include 301 and 331 which involve the gain or loss to shareholders. Stockholders, in most cases, affect management decisions since they are the ones that may be the determining factor in a divestment if the corporate charter requires that the divestment must receive the shareholders' prior approval.

An in-depth analysis of Sec. 331 may reveal that liquidation under this section may not be very costly to the organization. A review of the conditions for qualification under each section is reflected in Appendix A.

The "code requirement" as illustrated in the discussion of Sections 331, 332, and 334 provides a general awareness of the complexity of the tax analysis in a liquidation process. However, this complexity can be very technical and sensitive if the disposition of the business is a sale of stock rather than a liquidation. In addition, its complexity deepens if the operation under analysis is solvent and a foreign subsidiary.

Therefore, an analyst must compile a list of tax consequences that might face the parent company if the divestment is to take place with positive tax implications.

LIST OF TAX CONSIDERATIONS

Although a comprehensive list is necessary to review, it is always important that the tax department of the parent company be involved. Interpretation of certain sections, as noted earlier, can be further researched by the corporate tax experts, as they are the individuals who would respond to any tax question regarding the divestment, raised by the tax commissioner. In case of the absence of a tax department, the services of outside tax counsel should be sought. The attention of the financial analyst should be directed to:

1. Determining the basis for gain or loss in a divestment.

2. Calculating the portion of the fixed assets that would be treated as ordinary income due to the recapture of depreciation.

---

1   See Appendix A for the complete quotations from the Internal Revenue Code.

3. Reviewing the tax benefits associated with plant automation and renovation.

4. Reviewing the consequences of the sale of assets through installment and the financial tax impact of such a transaction.

5. Reviewing the liquidation of a segment of the business and the qualification that this may have regarding "partial liquidation" under the respective section of the IRC as amended.

6. Reviewing the requirement list for a tax-free reorganization.

7. Analyzing capital loss carry-overs from other subsidiaries and divisions.

8. Checking the time frame of the liquidation under the respective section of the code that qualifies the operation for a no-loss-nor-gain liquidation.

9. Reviewing the tax benefits resulting from the write-off of a guaranteed debt of the parent company.

10. Analyzing the equity base and the percentage of ownership of the parent company as well as the loss carry forward in the case of foreign subsidiaries.

11. Analyzing the potential liability for unpaid social security and other tax withholdings and the status of such liability after the consummation of the sale.

12. Reviewing the utilization of spin-off and split-up for a divestment without incurring any short-term tax liability to the stockholders.

Based on the items presented, it is evident that a corporation considering the divestment of any of its operations keep abreast of the changes in tax laws impacting divestment. The disposition of approved candidates must be established at an early date in order that a maximum effort be made to effect the divestment on a timely basis for tax purposes. The timing and the methods of divestments are the subject of Chapter 15, which covers the analysis of sale of stock versus liquidation, utilizing theory and case format.

CHAPTER 15

SALE OF STOCK VERSUS LIQUIDATION: THE CLOSING PROCESS

What factors should be considered in a divestment by sale of stock?

What factors should be considered in a divestment by liquidation?

What are the advantages of a voluntary liquidation?

What are the disadvantages of an involuntary liquidation?

Historical and projected financial data are essential factors in determining whether the sale of the firm as an ongoing entity is financially feasible, or whether terminating the business in a liquidation process has any advantage over the sale of stock. This advantage is measured in terms of net cash proceeds from the sale or liquidation along with the EPS impact on the parent company. In either case, the results of the financial analysis are based on the assumptions made by management.

BACKGROUND INFORMATION

A careful review of the background for the company under evaluation is recommended. This review should be part of the write-up and should include the percent (%) of ownership the parent company has in the operation. It should also cover the current products manufactured and the status and size of the facility as well as the number of employees currently on payroll. The number of employees should reflect the salary employees as well as the hourly employees, with an overall approximate average years of service.

The next step of the analysis should be concerned with the actual financial status of the operation. This should include:

1. Net sales (four years' history and current year estimated actual).

2. Profit after tax.

3. Percent of profit after tax to sales (ROS).

4. ROA.

5. A year-to-date actual balance sheet and a pro forma balance sheet covering the current period with an estimate of the remaining months prior to the divestment.

6. A projection of the next five years including the current fiscal year (FY).

Once this information is obtained, analyzed, and tabulated, then the analysis of each alternative should proceed.

SALE OF STOCK

The sale of stock analysis should include an estimate of the recovery of the parent company's equity. This should be done by estimating the net worth to be recovered at various levels of the book value. For example, assumptions of the recovery value in some cases may range from zero percent (0%) to one hundred percent (100%) of the book value depending on the operation under divestment study and the status of the economy at the time of divestment.

The calculation of the net loss or gain on the divested investment must be done in two separate side-by-side columns under each assumed percent of recovery. The first column should reflect the "tax effect" in order to calculate the tax benefits on the capital loss or tax payment on capital gain. The second column should reflect the financial impact on the corporation in terms of total net loss or gain from the sale of the investment and the impact this sale has on the EPS.

Further calculation should be concerned with the net cash flow inflow or outflow from the sale. This should take into consideration the following:

1. Proceeds from the sale of stock.

2. Reduction in parent company debt as a result of the divestment.

3. Miscellaneous closing costs.

4. The tax benefits on the loss or the tax payment on the capital gain realized.

To clarify the sale of stock analysis, a hypothetical case study of the corporation XYZ, parent company, and its subsidiary S & D, which is one hundred percent (100%) owned by XYZ, will be analyzed. XYZ is a U.S. multinational corporation with central offices in Chicago, Illinois, while S & D is a manufacturing operation located in Frankfurt, Germany.

CASE STUDY ANALYSIS

Background - A brief review of the S & D's history reveals its characteristic as a manufacturing plant producing hydraulic brakes used principally by the automotive vehicle industry. It was acquired one hundred percent (100%) by the XYZ Corporation in 1979 through the acquisition of all shares from Schmidt Brothers.

The facility occupied by S & D includes a 70,000-square-foot production space with an adjacent 3,000 foot cafeteria for its 150 employees thirty (30) salaried and one hundred twenty (120) hourly.

Actual financial status - S & D operated at a profit in 1999, 2000, 2002, and 2003, with a loss incurred in 2001. Table 15.1 shows the actual financial performance for the period 1999-2003 while Table 15.2 shows the year to date balance sheet and the pro forma balance sheet at the expected time of divestment.

Table 15.1

S&D Company
SUMMARY OF ACUTUAL SALE AND PROFITS
FY 1999–2003
(US $000)

	1999	2000	2001	2002	2003
Sales	$2100	$2300	$2500	$2530	$3300
Profit/(Loss) After Tax	$ 140	$ 250	$(250)	$ 100	$ 150
ROS	6.7%	10.9%	(10.0%)	4.0%	4.5%
Average Asset Base	$1100	$1600	$1700	$1400	$1500
ATO	1.9	1.4	1.5	1.8	2.2
ROA	12.7%	15.3%	–	7.2%	9.9%
Number of Employees	250	200	175	150	150

The following are the actual and the pro forma balance sheets of the operation under analysis:

Table 15.2

S&D
Balance Sheet
December 31, 2003
(US $000)

ASSETS	ACTUAL 7/31/03	PRO FORMA 12/31/03
Cash	$ 5	$ 10
Net Receivables Outside	671	650
Intercompany	3	0
Inventories	650	600
Prepaid Expense	6	3
Net Fixed Assets	287	275
Total Assets	**$1622**	**$1538**
Liabilities and Capital		
Equity	$ 365	$ 300
Account Payable Outside	169	150
Intercompany		
Debt Including Short & Long Term	575	546
Net Worth	513	542
Total Liabilities & Capital Equity	**$1622**	**$1538**

Financial Projection - The annual financial plan of operations for the FY 2003-2007 reflects the following summary of future sales and profits:

Table 15.3

S&D
Summary of Projected Sale and Profits
FY 2003-2007
($000)

	2003	2004	2005	2006	2007
Sales	$3300	$3600	$3900	$4200	$4500
Profit/(Loss) After Tax	$ 150	$ 153	$ 160	$ 168	$ 220
ROS	4.5%	4.3%	4.1%	4.0%	4.9%
Average Asset Base	$1500	$1700	$1850	$2100	$2250
ATO	2.2	2.1	2.1	2.0	2.0
ROA	9.9%	9.0%	8.6%	8.0%	9.8%

The long-range plan of S & D includes new product lines which have been incorporated in the sales forecast. Therefore, additional equipment would be needed which is expected to be financed through the Citigroup of New York, if the operation is to be retained. However, the decision has been made to divest S & D. What divestment approach should be taken? This would depend on the analysis of the net worth amount to be recovered.

Evaluation of the Sale of Stock - Under this alternative, the recovery of zero percent (0%), fifty percent (50%) and one hundred percent (100%) of the net worth of S & D are assumed in the analysis. Table 15.4 reflects the different recovery values, the tax benefits, the EPS impact, and the cash inflow or outflow from the sale. In determining the EPS impact, as a result of the sale, on the XYZ Corporation, a total number of 10,000,000 outstanding shares is used to arrive at the EPS figure.

Table 15.4

S & D
STOCK SALE ALTERNATIVE

(U.S. $000)

	Tax Effect	Book Effect	Tax Effect	Book Effect	Tax Effect	Book Effect
I. XYZ Profit/(Loss) on Investment						
Stock Sale	0	0	272	272	542	542
Investment	(600)*	(542)	(600)*	(542)	(600)*	(542)
Misc. Closing Cost	(50)	(50)	(50)	(50)	(50)	(50)
Goodwill write-off	(0)	(100)	(0)	(100)	(0)	(100)
Net Profit/(loss) Before Tax	(650)	(692)	(378)	(420)	(108)	(150)
Tax Benefits @ 30% Capital Loss Rate**	195	195	113	113	32	32
Net Profit/(loss) After Tax		(497)		(307)		(118)
Impact on XYZ EPS (After Tax)		(5.0)¢		(3.1)¢		(1.2)¢
II. Cash – Inflow/(Outflow)	0%		50%		100%	
Proceeds from Sale of Stock	$ 0		$272		$ 542	
Reduction in Short-term & Long-term debt	546		546		546	
Misc Closing Cost	(50)		(50)		(50)	
Tax Benefits	195		113		32	
Estimated Cash Flow including debt reduction	**$691**		**$881**		**$1070**	

*The $600,000 is the initial investment XYZ had in the S & D Company.
**The Capital Gain/Loss tax rate has been amended for corporations and this 30% rate is used for illustration purposes.

Based on the assumptions and facts presented in the analysis of the S & D Company, it is evident that the sale of stock would generate a negative impact on the EPS. Whether or not this negative impact is as sizable as the impact derived from the liquidation of S & D depends on further analysis of the liquidation alternative.

LIQUIDATION

Liquidation surfaces when there is no hope for the successful operation of a firm. However, it can be voluntary and involuntary. The analysis of S & D liquidation alternative is a voluntary one since it is the XYZ Corporation who is making the decision to liquidate.

Liquidation can be within the federal district court or it can be achieved outside the courts. "Outside the court" liquidation procedure involves a net worth of various steps that should be followed if the parent corporation does not or cannot guarantee the debt of the troubled operation. These steps are as follows:

1. A general assignment for the benefit of the creditors must be executed.

2. The debtor's assets should be transferred to a designated party elected by the creditors for the purpose of converting the assets into cash.

3. The designated party would liquidate the assets, pay the creditors and distribute the remaining funds to the stockholders.

In the case of S & D Company, the XYZ Corporation is expected to guarantee the debt and therefore XYZ would handle the liquidation process. Before such a liquidation can proceed, the financial advantages of its feasibility must be calculated.

Liquidation Analysis of the S & D Company - The non-recurring costs involved in the liquidation must be outlined. In this case, the liquidation costs included the following:

1. **Separation Costs** - A total of twelve (12) months of employees' salaries and wages should he provided as part of the liquidation. German law requires that for every year of service a month of pay must be given to the terminated employee as compensation. In addition, a special allowance required for mass termination of employees would account for an additional two months of pay.

2. **Lease Breaking Costs** - The lease agreement should be reviewed in line with the German law. For example, the annual rent of the building must be considered since the lease commitment expires on 12/31/2004. The

annual lease is at $200,000 which would place the company's rental liability at $300,000, considering that no sub-leasing could be achieved.

3. **Other Closing Costs** - These include the liquidation administrative cost, lease breaking cost on equipment and other unforeseen expenses resulting from liquidation.

The tabulation of the non-recurring closing costs as discussed is as shown in Table 15.5.

Table 15.5
S&D
Non-Recurring Closing Costs
(US $000)

Non-recurring Costs	$000
Separation Costs	$1,800
Lease Breaking Cost	300
Other Closing Costs	50
Total	**$2150**

In reviewing the 12/31/03 pro forma balance sheet, the analyst must utilize the assumptions and facts to arrive at a recovery figure. A fact may be that Mercedes Benz is interested in the company and would like to control the supply source of such products for its manufacturing plants, and therefore may desire to purchase the fixed assets. However, the assumptions may include different levels of recovery values for each of the assets. These assumptions are shown in Table 15.6.

Table 15.6

S&D

Assumptions Used in Calculating the Liquidation Alternative Percent of Recovery

Asset Category	% of Recovery on Book Value		
	A	**B**	**C**
Cash	100%	100%	100%
Receivables	100	100	100
Inventories	50	75	100
Prepaid Expense	0	0	0
Net Fixed Assets	50	75	100

Given these assumptions, the analyst should then calculate the liquidation alternative. These asset recovery percentages can be applied to the 12/31/03 balance sheet to arrive at the total sale value of the assets. Table 15.7 reflects these values.

Table 15.7

S&D

Asset Recovery Values
($000)

| | | Recovery Values | |
Asset Category	A	B	C
Cash	$10	$10	$10
Receivables	650	650	650
Inventories	300	450	600
Prepaid Expense	0	0	0
Total Current Assets	$ 960	$1110	$1260
Net Fixed Assets	138	206	275
Total Sale of Assets	**$1098**	**$1316**	**$1535**

Once the total sale of asset value is calculated, the analyst should determine the cash proceeds that would be realized from the liquidation under the assumptions utilized. Table 15.8 shows three different columns A, B, and C, with the cash proceeds under each assumption.

Table 15.8

S&D
CASH PROCEEDS AND INVESTMENTS NEEDED – LIQUIDATION
(US $000)

	Recovery Values		
	A	**B**	**C**
Total Sale of Assets	$ 1098	$ 1316	$ 1535
Less: Debt and Other Liabilities	(996)	(996)	(996)
Cash Proceeds Before Non-recurring Costs	$ 102	$ 320	$ 529
Less: Non-recurring Closing Costs	$ (2150)	$ (2150)	$ (2150)
Net Investment Needed for Liquidation	$(2048)	$(1830)	$(1611)

Further calculation should involve the tax benefits that Corporatiion XYZ must receive in this liquidation. This calculation is then based on the additional investment needed as well as the write-off of the original investment. Table 15.9 shows the tax benefits calculation. Please note that the tax rate used is not the actual tax rate but is used as a hypothetical rate for illustration purposes.

Table 15.9

S&D

TAX BENEFITS FROM LIQUIDATION

(US $000)

	A*	B*	C*
XYZ Original Investment	$ (600)	$ (600)	$ (600)
Additional Investment Required for Liquidation	$(2048)	$(1830)	$(1611)
Total Tax – loss	$(2648)	$(2430)	$(2211)
Tax Benefits Utilizing Average Corporate Tax Rate of 46%**	**$ 1218**	**$ 1118**	**$ 1017**

* See Table 15.6 for explanation.
**The corporate tax rate of 46% rate is used for illustration purposes. See the IRS Tax Table for rates since the rates are progressive and they level at 35% for income in excess of $18.3 million.

The tax benefits calculation should assist the analyst in deriving the cash flow figures from liquidation. These cash flow figures can be derived as shown in Table 15.10.

Table 15.10

S&D
CAST FROM LIQUIDATION
(US $000)

	A	**B**	**C**
Net Investment Needed for Liquidations (Table 15.8)	$(2048)	$(1830)	$(1611)
Tax Benefits To Be Realized from Liquidations (Table 15.9)	1218	1118	1017
Net Cash Flow from Liquidation Inflow/Outflow	**$ (830)**	**$ (712)**	**$ (594)**

The financial impact on the EPS of XYZ Corporation is important in the analysis process. Therefore, the evaluation of the book loss generated, based on the assumptions, must be calculated. The profit and loss from liquidation would then be based on the total profit or loss on the sale of the assets as well as the non-recurring closing costs and any other calculated tax savings resulting from the liquidation. This approach is shown in Table 15.11.

Table 15.11

S&D
IMPACT OF LIQUIDATION ON THE XYZ CORPORATION
(US $000)

Profit/(Loss) from Liquidation	**A**	**B**	**C**
Inventories	(300)	(150)	-0-
Prepaid Expense	(3)	(3)	(3)
Net Fixed Assets	(137)	(69)	-0-
Total Profit/(Loss) on Sale of Assets	$ (440)	$ (222)	$ (3)
Write-off of goodwill	(100)	(100)	(100)
Non-recurring Closing Costs	$(2150)	$(2150)	$(2150)
Tax Benefits	1218	1118	1017
Net Profit/(Loss)	$(1472)	$(1354)	$(1236)

Case Conclusion - The results of the negative EPS financial impact under the liquidation alternative are larger than those under the sale of stock. Therefore, the analyst should recommend that Corporation XYZ sell the S & D Company as an ongoing entity. This sale should be contingent to the transfer of all the S & D liabilities and loan guarantees from the XYZ Corporation to a third party (acquirer) thus releasing XYZ Corporation from all financial liabilities connected with the S & D Company.

Liquidation Advantages - The hypothetical case utilized showed the sale of stock as a better financial decision than the liquidation alternative. This cannot be taken as the most feasible approach to use in all circumstances. Usually, a corporation is unable to locate an acquirer for its ongoing operation and, therefore, is forced to liquidate. This type of liquidation as referred to earlier is noted as voluntary and is exercised outside the courts. Its advantages would include:

1. Lower legal fees.

2. Guaranteed debt by the parent company and agreement with the debtor on the assignee selected.

3. Ability of the parent company to search for potential buyers of the fixed assets.

4. Ability of the parent company to account for the liquidation in terms of

   a. how the assets should be disposed.

   b. the current balances of the debtors.

   c. the proceeds from liquidation.

   d. the cash disbursement.

   e. the expected tax savings under various alternatives, i.e., guaranteed debt approach versus no guarantee approach.

   f. the structuring of the statement of realization from liquidation reflecting the different financial schedules as illustrated in the tables in this chapter.

These are the advantages for liquidation outside the federal courts. Liquidation within the federal courts may mean bankruptcy and therefore is involuntary. This type can be very costly to an organization since the court usually appoints a referee to take over the operation and calls a meeting of the creditors. The creditors are then given the chance to appoint a trustee who will have the responsibility of liquidating the assets, paying the creditors, and distributing the remaining cash to the stockholders. This is totally done under the supervision of the courts and, therefore, must secure the payment of the IRS taxes along with court fees prior to the payment of claims. Cases further illustrating the liquidation process are shown in Part Six. However, prior to discussing these types of cases, a thorough discussion of Leveraged Buy-Out (LBO) is presented in the following chapters which are in Part Five.

PART FIVE

Leveraged Buy Out (LBO)

CHAPTER 16

LBO CONCEPT

What is an LBO?

Why do LBOs exist?

What is the main purpose of an LBO?

Does an LBO bring new life to management?

How does the financial deal work?

What happens to the existing shareholders?

Is there a conflict of interest on the part of management in pursuing an LBO?

LBO CONCEPT

Leveraged Buyout takes place when the management of a company or an outside raider tries to use the company's assets to buy it. This process centers around the funding of this type of acquisition for the purchase of a majority of ownership in the target company using equity and as much debt as is feasible. The goal of the acquirer, whether it is management or an outside raider, is to restructure the company and enhance it with the ultimate purpose of divesting it as a going entity or selling it in parts within a targeted period of time which can be usually two to five years, depending on the intended strategy. The main objective is to maximize the acquirer's return--thus producing a return in excess of that achieved by the average industry in which the acquisition is done. The method of using as much debt as practicable to purchase the majority ownership in a company allows the acquirer to leverage the return on equity (ROE) and consequently maximize it over and above the benchmark set.

The intention of the acquirer may vary depending on the design of the strategy. It may be set to acquire the majority of the common stock with the goal of liquidating or selling out some of the company's divisions or subsidiaries, subsequent to the acquisition, and keeping those products or divisions that may have synergy with the acquirer's operation. Leveraging debt as related to valuable assets makes this approach very lucrative to raiders.

In an LBO the raider analyzes the balance sheet mainly looking at cash and marketable securities. Subsequent to the analysis of the balance sheet, the raider will search for a potential investment banking company that will be able to handle such a deal. If the investment banking company, after reviewing the proposal from the raider, sees a potential, it will get busy in strategy design for financing such a venture.

Sometimes the raider's intention in a leveraged buyout is not clearly specified. Although raiders may paint a glorious picture of the outcome for management and the employees, their purpose may be to get rid of mediocre management and streamline the business focus with the intention of divesting part of the operation and paying a portion of the debt incurred in the acquisition process. Targeting a company and analyzing its assets, and mainly the current assets, is part of the technique used by the raiders. The working capital and especially the net working capital is of major interest to any of the raiders because the intention is an exit strategy that will complement the originally designed strategy of the acquisition. The figure below reflects the leverage approach of such a concept.

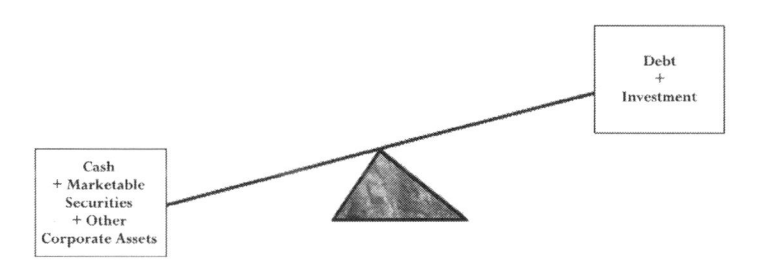

Figure 1: The LBO Concept

LBO STRUCTURE

How to structure an LBO is part of the strategic approach that an acquirer will follow. Most LBO firms utilize a mix of strategies. These strategies are typically employed to boost the ROE, the return on investment (ROI), or the return on capital invested. In order to illustrate this structural approach to LBO, let us use one of the major LBO acquisitions that was completed in the late eighties. In fact in 1988, a $24.6 billion acquisition of RJR Nabisco was orchestrated by the firm of Kohlberg, Kravis, and Roberts and Company referred to as KKR. Henry Kravis, the major designer of this acquisition strategy, went head to head with F. Ross Johnson, the Chief Executive Officer (CEO) of RJR Nabisco. The *Wall Street Journal* published a series of articles on this particular acquisition and later a film was introduced called *Barbarians at the Gate*, which depicted the process and the activities that had transpired, including the bidding war between the "management team" headed by F. Ross Johnson and the outside raider, KKR, headed by Henry Kravis[1]. The film was based on the book entitled *Barbarians at the Gate*, written by Brian Burrough and John Heylar and based on most of the articles published in the *Wall Street Journal*, as well as interviews with some of the people involved in this transaction. According to the literature covering articles and cases in the *Wall Street Journal*, *Financial Times*, and *Financial Analysts Journal*, the "management team" through their investment bankers, Shearson American Express, was able to offer the Board of Directors $75 per share when the stock was selling at $53 1/8. This put the market value of the company at seventeen billion dollars ($17 Billion), which was $5 Billion above its market capitalization at that point in time. When Charles Hugel, then Chairman of the Board of RJR Nabisco, received this offer from Ross Johnson, the RJR Board appointed a special committee of the board who immediately retained two financial advisors, Dillon Read and Lazard Freres in addition to retaining Peter Atkins' company. Also, the "special committee" selected Skadden, Arps, Slate, Meagher and Flom as legal counsel to guide and advise them on the legal steps that the RJR Board should take relative to dealing with this situation.

---

1   <u>Barbarians at the Gate.</u> dir. Glenn Jordan, with James Garner, Jonathan Pryce, and Peter Riegert, 107 min. Columbia Pictures, 1993. Videocassette.

Prior to the formal offer by the "management team," Johnson had approached Shearson American Express to handle the deal. It was Shearson American Express who put the deal together for Ross Johnson. Johnson's legal counsel in this project were Davis, Polk, & Wardell, while his lead bankers were City Bank and Bankers Trust. Although this deal was supposed to be a paved road for Ross Johnson, the RJR Board upon advice of their legal counsel issued a press release announcing the offer made by the "management team." This press release resulted in additional offers from KKR and First Boston, thus creating a pool of three bidders. The bids submitted included a combination of cash, preferred stock, and convertible preferred as well as convertible bonds.

First Boston's offer was disqualified because of the uncertainty associated with the tax benefits etc.. The two remaining offers were from KKR and the " management team." These offers were equivalent in value and were worth approximately $108.00/share.

In evaluating these two offers, the Special Committee of the Board made their recommendation to select KKR after deliberation and careful review of all the factors presented by the investment bankers. In weighing out the proposals, the Special Committee reviewed the details such as the Preferred-in-Kind (PIK) stock and the rates this stock was pegged to along with other items that would be of great interest to the shareholders.

The question that can be raised relative to the aforementioned decision concerns the details of the structure of the LBO transaction by the "management team" versus that of KKR. Was there a difference? If yes, was the outcome related to the offer as structured by Drexel, Burnham, Lambert (KKR Investment Bankers) versus Shearson American Express (the "management team" Investment Bankers)? Definitely, the composition of the offer made a difference in the evaluation process of the Special Committee. Here the business judgment rule and the fiduciary responsibility of the Board of Directors were important elements in the decision making process.

Although the steps in structuring this LBO transaction were the same type of steps followed by both investment bankers, the detailed content of the transaction was different, thus resulting in a preference of one over the other.

What are these steps used in the LBO process? The LBO steps used in the acquisition process of any publicly held company can be similar to those listed below:

1. **Research the Target Company**: In researching the target company the management team/acquirer must make sure that the cash and marketable securities along with the corporate assets can be used to fund the buyout. In the case of RJR Nabisco, the "management team" had an advantage over KKR because they had accessibility to audited and non-audited statements

and were able to have Shearson American Express review internal financial reports that helped them put the initial $17 Billion offer together.

2. **Evalute the Management Group**: In reviewing top management capabilities, the acquirer must look at the strengths of the management team and how these strengths could move the target company forward. Also, a careful review of those weak elements must be done, and a list of who should be terminated should be formulated.

3. **Recruit an Experienced LBO Consultant**: In recruiting the consulting firm, careful review of the staff's experience in negotiation must be done. Negotiating the LBO deal is an important part in the success of the LBO transaction.

4. **Select an Experienced Investment Banker**: Selection of an investment banker is very important because it should be a company with experienced leveraged buyout, which should be willing to work with the accounting and legal teams of the acquirer.

5. **Assemble an Acquistion Team**: This team should be composed of financial advisors, legal advisors, accountants, and investment bankers.

6. **Use Parking in the LBO Process**: Acquire up to 4.99% of the stock and colaborate with the investment bankers and other friendly investors to each acquire up to 4.99% of the target company for investment purposes. (Once a company acquires 5% or more, they must file a 13 D Schedule with the SEC within 10 days of the acquisition event.)

7. **Contact the Management Group through the Consultant Relative to an LBO**: In case of an LBO by the top management group, the contact should be made with the Chairman of the Board who in turn will bring it to the attention of the Board of Directors of the Target Company. If the Board resists, management should immediately file a 13 D schedule with the SEC and have all the support group tender their shares at the offered stock price.

Utilizing the aforementioned steps in the LBO process can simplify the raider's task in a takeover activity. Takeover and LBO go hand in hand in today's business environment. Their complexities are part of corporate management activities that are occupying part of top management's time in planning the defensive mechanisms that will reduce the chance of an LBO by a potential raider. These complexities and managerial activities are discussed in the following chapter.

CHAPTER 17

LBO ACTIVITIES AND COMPLEXITIES

Who is making the deal?

What are the US activities vs. that of the European in LBOs?

What are some of the benchmark LBOs in the US market?

Does management of the target company make or break the deal?

Buyout Activities

The LBO activities have been stimulated by three elements in the environment. These elements include, (1) the availability of cash in the accounts of institutional investors who are seeking a higher return, (2) an increase in the number of investment bankers who are searching for transactions to handle, and (3) an economy that has been fueled by debt and stable low interest rates. Recent deals involved cross-border acquisitions, mainly with US companies being targeted by the United Kingdom (UK) and Canadian companies, as well as companies from France, Germany, and Japan. Collectively, these five countries have represented more than 60% of the cross-border acquisitions[1]. The number of European transactions dealing with mergers, acquisitions, and LBOs in 2005 was about 1,047 with the total value of these transactions reaching a record of 125.3 billion Euros/an equivalent of $163 billion (US dollars). This trend, which has been supported by European banks' willingness to leverage transactions, as well as investment bankers going after raising larger capital by inticing the appetite of institutional investors for higher return, has been the fueling factor in these buyout activities.

France, for example, in 2005 had a record year for French private equity. Not only did the French complete 133 LBOs, but in 2005 it was an outstanding year for the French to have a total value of a private equity investment, which was the highest ever in the history of their country. At the close of the 2005 year, the total value of private equity LBOs for France stood at 20.6 billion Euros or approximately $27 billion US.[2]

Germany, compared with the UK and France, recorded a 13.9 billion Euros in buyouts or approximately $18.1 billion. While these developments and the mega deals have taken place in overseas markets and across borders, it is important to note that in 2004, one in every eight US companies sold was acquired by a foreign company.[3]

As it is noted, U S Companies are LBO targets especially when their balance sheets reflect healthy financial positions. Raiders and company executives are usually part of a deal, or they may be at odds with one another. Just as this book was being completed, *Barron's* noted in its July 9th, 2007 issue that FedEx Corporation could become a target for private equity buyers. The reason given by Barron was that of FedEx's modest valuation and turnaround potential. According to Barron's, FedEx is valued at about 6 times the expected 2008 earnings before interest, taxes, depreciation, and amortization (EBITDA).[4] The market capitalization of

---

1   Thornton, Grant. *Dealmaker.* Vol. 2, No. 1. Summer 2005. July 16, 2007 www.GrantThornton.com/
2   Blees, Wietske and Lisa Stuart. Eds. *2005: An Overview of the European Buyout Market.* Incisive Media Investments Ltd. May 2006.
3   Ibid.
4   "FedEx Could Lure Private Equity Interest." *Barron's.* 8 July 2007. 24 July 2007 http://www.bnet.com/2407-13071_23-93774.html

FedEx is $35 billion. With the potential to lower capital expenditures and the opportunity to spare Kinko's, the attraction for buyout firms is gigantic.

Leveraged buyouts, as stated earlier, have been fueled by private equity funds. Companies that go after LBOs are looking at target firms with high leverage that will help them get the financial backing to complete the LBO transaction. How complex is this process and how is it achieved?

Complexities of the LBO Process

As noted earlier in this chapter, the equity firms are creating the heat in the LBO market. For example, KKR is adding the world's largest credit card payment company to its list of acquisitions by proceeding with an LBO of First Data, a Colorado-based company. According to Forbes.com, KKR will pay $34 per share, ie. 26.4% premium over the Friday's closing price.[5] First data.com stated that the transaction is valued at $29 billion. In addition, it stated that the agreement was unanimously approved by First Data's Board of Directors, based upon the recommendation of the Strategic Review Committee, which was composed of three independent directors.[6]

How does KKR plan to finance this acquisition? KKR is using Simpson Thatcher and Bartlett LLP as their legal advisors. KKR also has a commitment for using the debt financing from Citigroup, Credit Suisse, Deutsche Bank, HSBC, Lehman Brothers, Goldman Sachs, and Merrill Lynch. These investment bankers will also act as financial advisors, and the transaction will be subject to customary terms and conditions.[7] KKR intends to pay $29 billion including the assumption of $2 billion in debt. The financing of this buyout will involve a $16 billion credit consisting of a six-year covenant-lite revolver and a seven year covenant-lite term Loan B. In addition, the transaction will include the issuance of $8 billion in junk bonds and $5 ½ billion of senior unsecured notes, as well as $2 ½ billion dollars of senior subordinate notes as noted in First Data's proxy statement. Based on this transaction structure, Standard and Poor (S&P) lowered First Data's credit rating to B+. The analyst at S & P cautioned that less stringent loan covenants would result in lower recovery.[8]

---

5   Farrell, Andrew. "KKR Buying First Data for $29B." Forbes.com. 2 April 2007. 24 July 2007. http://www.forbes.com/markets/2007/04/02
6   "First Data to Be Acquired by KKR." *First Data Corp*. 2 April 2007. 24 July 2007. http://news.firstdatacorp.com/news
7   Ibid.
8   Morcroft, Greg. "S&P Sees Bad End for Many Leveraged Loans." MarketWatch. 16 July 2007. 24 July 2007. http://www.marketwatch.com/news/story

It seems from the financial literature that the credit ratings by S&P, Moody's, and other credit rating agencies have reflected a downgrading for First Data with all concerned, placing the company on credit watch.

According to S&P, covenant lite loans have become popular lately with more than 80% rated in the B class.[9] This type of financing is risky because the borrowing corporation can decrease in value before the lender can intervene—thus ending with a business/corporation which has a minimum value of assets that does not cover the debt owed to the lender. The covenant lite loan does not provide the lender the opportunity to take remedial actions based on "maintenance" covenants but rather uses the "incurring" covenant which does not consider benchmarking of performance but rather utilizes the notation of "incurring" additional debt before the lender can intervene. Therefore, the financing of LBO transactions as they are currently structured are a risk to the lender and may lead the investment bankers to reinvent the history of junk bonds with covenant-lite loans of today.

In earlier chapters, the methods of evaluating acquisitions for takeovers or friendly mergers were discussed. However, for LBO purposes, it is essential to look at the detailed structure of financing the acquisition and how the payment would be made. Is it strictly in cash or a combination of cash and preferred stock or subordinate debt? Whatever the structure is, it is important to calculate the weighted average cost of capital (WACC). This WACC must be compared to the expected rate of return. This expected rate of return must be based on the exit strategy of the acquiring company and might include the possible liquidation/sale of the divisions or subsidiaries that were part of the acquisition and were evaluated as potential cash flow generators for the reduction of debt incurred by the LBO process. In the case of KKR's acquisition of First Data, the company determined price of $34/share is based on the amount of debt that KKR would be able to structure into this transaction. This KKR acquisition model includes assumptions of future cash flows and the exit value that will result in the expected rate of return. Utilizing this expected rate of return and developing future cash flows with a cash residual value in five to ten years at the time of the divestment would be the approach that LBO raiders undertake as part of the LBO process.

Details of these methods are presented and illustrated in Chapter 8 of this text. However, Part Three of the book covers the target identification and purchase price determination utilizing the present value of future cash flows as well as the price earning multiple and the networth approach. Relative to the method of financing, a thorough discussion of debt financing is given with alternative equity options which can be utilized by the acquirer, depending on its financial status and the WACC. While Part Three deals with acquisition considerations, Part Four focuses on the divestment process which is part of the LBO strategy and discusses details of the methods used. Retention versus divestiture is discussed and the financial analyst recommendations to selling subsidiaries by spin-off, split-off, or split-up are clearly illustrated. These factors of acquisition through debt financing and the ultimate reduction of the debt generated through the LBO process are part of most LBOs' objectives

---

9 Ibid.

as well as LBOs' exit strategies. These objectives are further illustrated in Part Six which is entitled "Cases in Acquisitions and Divestments."

PART SIX
Cases

Activities in Acquisitions, Divestments, and LBOs

Mergers, takeovers, or LBOs outcomes are the product of the objective set by the acquirer. The intention of acquiring and then divesting can be a combined objective that is related to the designed strategy of the acquirers' layout at the beginning of such a process. In this section of the book, two cases are presented. One is a hypothetical case dealing with a divestiture, and the other is a real life case dealing with an acquisition/merger.

In evaluating any company for an acquisition, it is recommended that the following outline be used in writing up a report to the corporate board of directors in order to assist board members in understanding the objectives of the acquisition as well as the impact that the acquisition will have on the acquirer.

Suggested Format for Case Writeup

I. Case Highlights

    A. Name of Related Parties
    B. Date of Acquisition or Divestiture
    C. Amount of Purchase Price
    D. State of Incorporation

II. Background Information

    A. Previously Owned Facilities
    B. Organizational Objectives
    C. Services Provided

III. Management's Position

    A. Company Growth: How does the company being acquired fit into the long range plans of the acquirer?
    B. Management strengths and weaknesses of the target company
    C. Profit and Loss Comparisons: Consolidated Statements reflecting the purchase transaction.

IV. Stated Criteria for the Acquisition

    A. Purchase Price
    B. Goodwill
    C. Financing
    D. Transaction Structure: This transaction structure should be in line with III.B.

V. Contingencies

   A. Guarantees (if any) by the Acquirer given to the Bureau of Corporation (seller's state of incorporation) that would retain its offices and management
   B. Status of Movement of Assets
   C. Other (specify)

CASE 1
MANUFACTURER'S CORPORATION
DIVESTMENT CASE STUDY

BACKGROUND INFORMATION

The Electrodynamics Company was originally acquired in September of 2000 when Manufacturers Corporation acquired all of the shares of the stock. The acquisition was intended to strengthen one of the product lines and move Manufacturers from a loss position into a profit situation. The acquisition, in fact, resulted in strengthening a series of product lines including the dynamic control as well as the airport detective products. Although the acquisition was financed partially through debt, the improvement in the profit picture and the restriction in the payment of dividends reflected a continual decrease in the debt-to-equity ratio.

In an effort to comply with the FTC order to divest the Electrodynamic Company, Manufacturers Corporation's stockholders were assured in the 2003 proxy statement that the best interests of the shareholders would be of uppermost importance when the selection of the divestment criteria were made.

MANAGEMENT'S POSITION

Corporate management, having experienced an increase in earnings per share, was reluctant to divest Electrodynamics. However, the General Counsel of the Corporation had carefully reviewed the original submission to the FTC as well as to the SEC and advised management that they must divest the subsidiary and avoid further confrontation with the FTC and the U.S. Department of Justice.

Top management, having accepted the corporate general counsel's advice, decided to divest the Electrodynamic subsidiary. The forms of divestments considered were:

   (1) Spin-off of Electrodynamics by giving 1/3 share for each share owned in Manufacturers.

(2) A sale of Electrodynamics as an on-going entity to another corporation.

(3) A public offering of Electrodynamics' shares.

(4) A sale of Electrodynamics' assets, in other terms the liquidation of the Electrodynamic Company.

FINANCIAL STATUS

As a financial analyst employed by Manufacturers Corporation, you were asked to recommend one of the above alternatives that will be in the best interest of the shareholders. The following financial data were given to you.

(1) Income Statements, fiscal year 2004, for Manufacturers Corporation and Electrodynamics. Exhibits I and II.

(2) Balance Sheets, fiscal year 2004, for Manufacturers Corporation and Electrodynamics. Exhibits III and IV.

SUGGESTED NOTES

(1) FY is from October 1 to September 31.

(2) Impact on EPS must be shown.

(3) Analysis of alternatives must consider tax implications.

(4) Cash flow should be used in determining sale price.

(5) P/E of Manufacturers Corporation prior to acquisition was 2.0 and in 2004 it reached a 6.0.

(6) Alternative selected must be in line with SEC requirements and should satisfy FTC rules.

EXHIBIT I
MANUFACTURERS CORPORATION
INCOME STATEMENT
FY 2004

($000)

Net Sales (Excluding Intra- and Inter-Company)		$575,608
Costs and expenses:		
Cost of goods sold	$438,222	
Selling, adm., and general expense	80,301	
Provision for bad debt	1,779	
Depreciation	28,553	548,855
Gross Profit		26,753
Other Income		951
		$27,704
Less: Interest Expense		15,508
Income from Operation		$12,196
Taxes		4,847
Net income available to stockholder		**$ 7,349**
EPS		$7.35

EXHIBIT II
ELECTRODYNAMICS COMPANY
INCOME STATEMENT
FY 2004
($000)

Net Sales		$275,000
Cost and Expenses:		
Cost of goods sold	$206,250	
Selling & Adm. Exp.	32,000	
Provision for bad debt	850	
Depreciation	12,530	251,630
Gross Profit		$23,370
Less: Interest Expense		5,543
Net Income Before Taxes		$ 17,827
Less: Central Office Expense @ 3%		8,250
Net Income Before Taxes & After COE		**$ 9,577**

EXHIBIT III
MANUFACTURERS CORPORATION
CONSOLIDATED BALANCE SHEET
FY 2004
($000)

Assets		Liabilities & Capital Equity	
Current Assets:		Current Liabilities:	
Cash	$ 15,644	A/P	$ 30,000
A/R	70,844	Notes Payable	40,743
Inventories	147,216	Accrued Wages	5,395
Prepaid Expense	4,850	Accrued Taxes	1,212
Total Current Assets	$238,554		
		Other Current Liab.	19,604
Net Fixed Assets $96,954	$112,513	Total Current Liab.	
Other Assets	26,178	Long-Term Debt	130,005
Total Assets	**$377,245**	Other Long-Term Liabilities	30,329
		Total Long-Term Liabilities	**$160,334**
		Capital Equity	216,911
		Total Liabilities & cr CapitalEquity	**$377,245**

EXHIBIT IV
ELECTRODYNAMICS COMPANY
BALANCE SHEET
FY 2004
($000)

Asset		Liabilities & Capital Equity	
Current Assets:		Current Liabilities:	
Cash	$5,000	A/P	$10,000
A/R	25,550	Notes Payable	10,740
Inventories	62,150	Interco. Pay.	10,500
Prepaid Expense	800	Other Current Liab.	11,300
Total Current Assets	$93,500	Total Current Liab.	$47,540
		Long-term Debt	$50,130
		Other Long-term Liab.	5,300
Net Fixed Assets	$51,230	Total Long-term	$55,430
Other Assets	5,700	Net Worth	52,460
Total Assets	**$150,430**	Tot. Liab. & Cap. Equ.	**$150,430**

CASE 2
Chevron's Acquisition of Unocal
Acquisition Case Study

CASE HIGHLIGHTS

According to the *Wall Street Journal* in April of 2007, Chevron Corporation made an offer to acquire Unocal Corporation at $69.00 in cash or 1.03 shares of Chevron's stock or a combination of cash plus Chevron's shares. The combination offer included $27.60 in cash and 0.618 shares of Chevron's stock. The Chevron Chairman and Chief Executive Officer (CEO) expressed Chevron's strategic intention by stating that this acquisition will create synergy and enhance organizational capabilities, thus creating an ability to produce 2.8 million barrel of oil daily. Furthermore, he stated that Chevron's reserves will increase by approximately fifteen percent (15%) and reduce production which will give Chevron a competitive edge over other oil companies.

BACKGROUND

According to Chevron's Shareholder's report, Chevron claims to be one of the largest integrated energy companies. Headquartered in San Ramon, CA, it conducts business in about 180 countries. On September 11, 2006, David O'Reilly decided to pay approximately $16.4 billion for rival, Unocal and its oil resources, according to David Lazarus of the *San Francisco Chronicle*. Lazarus stated that O'Reilly knows the world oil market and is prepared to gamble more than $16 billion dollars at oil prices. Unocal, on the other hand, is the parent company of Union Oil Company of California, which was incorporated in 1890 in California. Virtually, it does business as Unocal and its subsidiaries. It sold its retail operations using the trademark, Union 76, to Tosco in 1997.

In April 2005, Unocal agreed to merge with Chevron. However, in June of 2005, the China Offshore Oil Corporation (CNOOC) made a rival $18.5 billion bid for its stock. CNOOC is a state-owned enterprise of the People's Republic of China and had the backing of the Chinese government. The United States House of Representatives passed a nonbinding resolution urging President George W. Bush to review the bid, citing national security concern. According to the *Wall Street Journal*, on July 19, 2005, the Unocal-Chevron merger was accepted and on August 10, 2005, the merger was completed. The Chineese were out of the picture on this transaction.

ACQUISITION OBJECTIVES

In analyzing this particular acquisition, the questions relative to Chevron's strategic intent of acquiring Unocal can be as follows:

1. Was Chevron acquiring the customer base?

2. Was it acquiring Unocal name brands?

3. Was it acquiring management talent?

4. What was the product synergy of this acquisition?

5. Was Chevron intending to divest any of Unocal's subsidiaries to reduce the debt generated by this acquisition?

6. What were Chevron's top management objectives relative to Unocal's objectives and management qualifications?

7. Were the objectives of this acquisition to reduce cost through a combination of similar functions, thus reducing manpower and duplication of operations?

SUGGESTED READINGS

After reviewing this brief description of this acquisition, you are to consult the following reports and agencies:

1. Shareholders' Report of Chevron available on the web subsequent to the merger.

2. Shareholders' Report of Unocal 2005, prior to the merger, SEC archives.

3. *Wall Street Journal* articles of April, July, and August 2005.

4. *Standard and Poor*.

5. *Value Line Reports*.

6. *BusinessWeek*

7. Securities Exchange Commission, filed reports, Washington, D.C., available through
EDGAR at www.sec.gov/

8. Form 10K for both corporations prior to the merger.

CASES

9. *Forbes*

10. *Dun and Bradstreet Reports.*

11. State Laws of the state of incorporation of both corporations.

12. Any other periodicals and brokers' agencies reports that would be helpful in putting this case together.

CONSIDERATIONS IN FINANCIAL EVALUATION

The analysis of this case must be completed and then rewritten in a formal report to be handed to the Chairman of the Board of Chevron's Corporation. In writing this report you will need to incorporate the answers to the following questions:

1. How did Chevron choose Unocal?

2. How was the price of $69 in cash or 1.03 shares of Chevron stock determined?

3. How and where did the negotiation take place? Who was the initial negotiator of this process?

4. Is there any legal consideration that each company must carefully review?

5. How do statutory laws impact this merger?

6. What is the type of transaction that is generated by this acquisition? Is there any goodwill generated? If there is, how and on whose financial records would this goodwill appear?

7. What are the tax consequences impacting this merger?

8. What financial implication would this acquisition have on Chevron, taking into consideration the pre-merger shareholders' report?

9. How does the William Bill impact this merger?

10. What should the tax objective of Chevron be in this case?

11. What should Chevron include in the acquisition contract and why?

12. Explain the closing and the post-closing process involved in this transaction.

**APPENDICES
A, B, & C**

APPENDIX A
INTERNAL REVENUE CODE

PORTIONS OF SECTIONS 331, 332, 333, 334, 337, 341, 351, 362, AND 368 AS RELATED TO ACQUISITION AND DIVESTMENT

(For further details, consult the Internal Revenue Code. Copies can be obtained by writing to the Superintendent of Government Documents, Washington, D.C. 20402, or to Prentice-Hall, Inc., or West Publishing /Thomson Business or Commerce Clearing House or visit http://www.fourmilab.ch/ustax/www/contents.html .)

SEC. 331. GAIN OR LOSS TO SHAREHOLDERS IN CORPORATE LIQUIDATIONS.

    (a) Distributions in Complete Liquidation Treated as Exchanges.
Amounts a shareholder receives in a distribution in complete liquidation of a corporation will be treated as total payment in exchange for the stock.

    (b) Nonapplication of Section 301.
Section 301 (relating to effects on shareholder of distributions of property) will not apply to any distribution of property (except for a distribution referred to in Sec. 316 (b) Paragraph (2) (B) in complete liquidation.

SEC 332. COMPLETE LIQUIDATIONS OF SUBSIDIARIES.

    (a) General Rule. - Neither gain nor loss will be recognized by a corporation on the receipt of property distributed in complete liquidation of another corporation.

    (b) Liquidations to Which Section Applies. - For purposes of subsection (a), a distribution will he considered in complete liquidation only if the following conditions prevail -

        (1) the corporation receiving the property was, on the date the plan of liquidation was adopted, and has continually been until the receipt of the property, the owner of stock (in such other corporation) possessing 80 percent or more of the total combined voting power of all classes of stock entitled to vote and the owner of 80 percent or more of the total number of shares of all other classes of stock (with the exception of nonvoting stock which is limited and preferred as to dividends); and either

(2) the distribution is by the other corporation in total cancellation or redemption of all its stock, and the property transfer occurs within the taxable year; in such case the shareholders' adoption of the resolution under which is authorized the distribution of all the assets of the corporation in total cancellation or redemption of all its stock will be considered to be an adoption of a plan of a liquidation plan, although no time for the completion of the property transfer is specified in the resolution, or

(3) the distribution is one of a series of distributions by the other corporation in total cancellation or redemption of its total stock in accordance with a liquidation plan under which the transfer of the total property under the liquidation is to be accomplished within 3 years from the end of the taxable year during which is made the first of the series of distributions under the plan, with the exception that if the transfer is not finished within the period, or if the taxpayer does not continue to be qualified under paragraph (1) until the finish of the transfer, no distribution under the plan will he considered to be a distribution in complete liquidation.

If the transfer of the total property is not completed during the taxable year, the Secretary may require of the taxpayer a bond or waiver of the statute of limitations on assessment/collection, as determined to be necessary to insure, if the property transfer is not completed within a 3-year period, or if the taxpayer does not continue to be qualified according to paragraph (1) until the completion of the transfer, the assessment and collection of the total income taxes then imposed by law for such taxable year or subsequent taxable years, to the extent applicable to property so received. A distribution otherwise constituting a distribution in total liquidation within the meaning of this subsection will not be considered as such a distribution simply because it does not constitute a distribution or liquidation within the meaning of the corporate law under which the distribution is made; and according to this subsection a transfer of property of such other corporation to the taxpayer shall not he considered as not constituting a distribution (or one of a series of distributions) in complete cancellation or redemption of the total stock of the other corporation, merely because the carrying out of the plan involves (A) the transfer under the plan to the taxpayer by the other corporation of property, not attributable to shares owned by the taxpayer, on an exchange described in section 361, and (B) the total cancellation or redemption under the plan, as a result of exchanges described in section 354, of the shares not owned by the taxpayer.

(REPEALED) [(c)   Special Rule for Indebtedness of Subsidiary to Parent. - If -

(1) a corporation is liquidated and subsection (a) applies to the liquidation, and

(2) on the adoption date of the liquidation plan, the corporation was indebted to the corporation which meets the 80 percent stock ownership requirements specified in subsection (b),then neither gain nor loss will be recognized to the corporation so indebted due to the transfer of property in satisfaction of such indebtedness.]

SEC. 333. * [ELECTION AS TO RECOGNITION OF GAIN IN CERTAIN LIQUIDATIONS.
(Sec. 333. Repealed. Pub. L. 99-514, title VI, Sec. 631(e)(3), Oct. 22, 1986, 100 Stat. 2273)

(a) General Rule. -In the case of property distributed in total liquidation of a domestic corporation (other than a collapsible corporation to which section 341(a) applies, if * SEC 333 Paragraphs (a) through (f) was repealed by SEC 631 Paragraph (e) (3).

(1) the liquidation is made in pursuance of a liquidation plan which has been adopted, and

(2) the distribution is in complete cancellation or redemption of all the stock, and the transfer of all the property under the liquidation occurs within some one calendar month, then each qualified electing shareholder (as defined in subsection (c) gain on the shares owned by that share-holder at the time of the adoption of the plan of liquidation shall be recognized only to the extent provided in (e) and (f) subsections.

(b) Excluded Corporation. - For purposes of this section, the term "excluded corporation" means a corporation which was the owner of stock possessing 5 percent or more of the total combined voting power of all classes of stock entitled to vote on the adoption of such a plan -- between the dates January 1, and the date of the adoption of the plan of liquidation, both dates inclusive.

(c) Qualified Electing Shareholders. - In this section, the term "qualified electing shareholder" means a shareholder (other than an excluded corporation) of any class of stock (whether or not entitled to vote on the adoption of the liquidation plan) who is a shareholder at the time the plan is adopted, and whose written election to have the benefits of subsection (a) has been made and filed in accordance with subsection (d), but -

(1) in the case of a shareholder other than a corporation, only if elections which have been written have been so filed by shareholders (other than corporations) who at the time of the adoption of the plan for liquidation are owners of stock possessing at least 80 percent of the total combined voting power (exclusive of voting power possessed by stock owned by corporations) of all classes of stock entitled to vote on the adoption of such a liquidation plan; or

(2) in the case of a shareholder which is a corporation, only if written elections have been filed by shareholders of the corporation (other than an excluded corporation) which at the time of such a liquidation plan is adopted, are owners of stock possessing at least 80 percent of the total combined voting power (exclusive of voting power possessed by stock owned by an excluded corporation and by shareholders who are not corporations) of all classes of stock entitled to vote on the adoption of such a liquidation plan.

(d) Making and Filing of Elections. -The written elections which were referred to in subsection (c) must be filed so as to not be in contravention of regulations prescribed by the Secretary. The filing must be within 30 days after the date of the adoption of the liquidation plan.

(e) Noncorporate Shareholders. -In the case of a qualified electing shareholder other than a corporation

(1) There will be recognized, and treated as a dividend, the amount of the gain which is not in excess of his ratable share of the earnings and profits of the corporation accumulated after February 28, 1913, with such earnings and profits to be determined as of the close of the month in which the liquidation transfer occurred under subsection (a), but without diminution by reason of distributions made during such month; but by including in the computation thereof all the amounts accrued up to the date on which the transfer is completed of all the property under the liquidation; and

(2) there will be recognized and treated as short-term or long-term capital gain, as the case may be, the amount of the remainder of the gain which is not in excess of the amount by which the value of that portion of the assets received by him which consists of money, or of stock or securities acquired by the corporation after December 31, 1953, exceeds his ratable share of such earnings and profits.

(f) Corporate Shareholders. -In the case of a qualified electing shareholder which is a corporation, the gain will be recognized only to the extent of the greater of the two following -

(1) the portion of the assets received by it consisting of money, or of stock or securities acquired by the liquidating corporation after December 31, 1953; or

(2) its ratable share of the earnings and profits of the liquidating corporation accumulated after February 8, 1913, such earnings and profits to be determined as of the close of the month in which the liquidation transfer occurred under subsection (a) (2), but without diminution by reason of distributions made during such month; but by including in the computation all amounts accrued up to the date on which the transfer of all the property under the liquidation is completed.] REPEALED

SEC. 334. BASIS OF PROPERTY RECEIVED IN LIQUIDATIONS.

(a) General Rule. if property is received in a distribution which is in complete liquidation (other than a distribution to which section 333 applies and if gain or loss is recognized on the receipt of such property, then the basis of the property in the hands of the distributee shall be the fair market value of the property at the time of the distribution.

(b) Liquidation of Subsidiary.

>(1) Distribution in complete liquidation. - If property is received by a corporation in a distribution in a complete liquidation to which section 332(a) applies, the basis of the property in the hands of the distributee will be the same as it would be in the hands of the transferor.

>(2) Transfers to which section 332 (c) applies. - If property is received by a corporation in a transfer to which section 332 (c) applies, the basis of the property in the hands of the transferee will be the same as it would be in the hands of the transferor.

SEC. 337. [GAIN OR LOSS ON SALES OR EXCHANGES IN CONNECTION WITH CERTAIN LIQUIDATIONS.

(a) General Rule. - If within the 12-month period beginning on the date on which a corporation adopts a plan of total liquidation, all of the assets of the corporation are distributed in complete liquidation, less assets retained to meet claims, then no gain or loss shall be recognized to such corporation from the sale or exchange by it of property within such 12-month period.

(b) Property Defined.

>(1) In general. - For purposes of subsection (a), the term "property" does not include

>>(A) stock in trade of the corporation, or other property of a kind which would improperly be included in the inventory of the corporation if on hand at the close of the taxable year, and property held by the corporation mainly for sales to customers in the ordinary course of its business or trade;

>>(B) installment obligations acquired in respect of the sale or exchange (without regard to whether such sale or exchange occurred before, on, or after the date of the adoption of the plan referred to in subsection (a) of stock in trade or other property described in subparagraph (A) of this paragraph, and

(C) installment obligations acquired in respect of property (other than property described in subparagraph (A) sold or exchanged before the date of the adoption of such a liquidation plan.

(2) Nonrecognition with respect to any property in certain cases. - Notwithstanding paragraph (1) of this subsection, if substantially all of the property described in subparagraph (A) of such paragraph (1) which is attributable to a business or trade of the corporation is, in accordance with this section, sold or exchanged to one person in one transaction, then for purposes of subsection (a) the term "property" includes -

(A) such property thus sold or exchanged, and

(B) installment obligations acquired in respect of such sale or exchange.

(c) Limitations. -

(1) Collapsible corporations and liquidations to which section 333 applies. - This section shall not apply to any sale or exchange –

(A) made by a collapsible corporation (as defined in section 34 (b), or

(B) following the adoption of a plan of total liquidation, if section 333 applies with respect to such liquidation.

(2) Liquidations to which section 332 applies. - In the case of any sale or exchange following the adoption of a plan of total liquidation, if section 332 applies with respect to such liquidation, this section shall not apply.

(3) Special rule for affiliated group.

(A) In general. Paragraph (2) shall not apply to a sale or exchange by a corporation (hereinafter in this paragraph referred to as the "selling corporation") if

(i) within the 12-month period beginning on the date of the adoption of a plan of total liquidation by the selling corporation, the selling corporation and each distributee corporation is completely liquidated, and
(ii) none of the complete liquidations referred to in clause d) is a liquidation with respect to which section 333 applies.

(B) Definitions. - For purposes of subparagraph (A) -

(i) The term "distributee corporation" means a corporation in the chain of including collapsible corporations to which the selling corporation or a corporation above the selling corporation in such chain makes a distribution in total liquidation within the 12-month period referred to in subparagraph (A)(i).

(ii) The term "chain if inclusible corporations" includes, in the case of any distribution, any corporation which (at the time of distribution) is in a chain of inclusible corporations for purposes of section 1504 (a) (determined without regard to the exceptions contained in section 1904(b), such term include, where appropriate, the common parent corporation.

(d) Special Rule for certain Minority Shareholders. - If a corporation adopts a plan of total liquidation, and if subsection (a) does not apply to sales or exchanges of property by the corporation, solely by reason of the application of subsection (c) (2), then for the first taxable year of any shareholder (other than a corporation which meets the 80 percent stock ownership requirement specified in section 332(b) 1 in which he receives a distribution in complete liquidation -

(1) the amount realized by such a shareholder on the distribution shall be increased by his proportionate share of the amount by which the tax imposed by this subtitle on such corporation would have been reduced if subsection (c)(2) had not been applicable, and

(2) for purposes of this title, such a shareholder shall be deemed to have paid, on the last day prescribed by law for the payment of the tax imposed by this subtitle on such shareholder for such taxable year, an amount of tax equal to the amount of the increase described in paragraph (1).

(e) Special Rule for Involuntary Conversions. - If -

(1) there is an involuntary conversion (within the meaning of section 1033) of property of a distributing corporation and there is a total liquidation of such corporation which qualifies under subsection (a),

(2) the disposition of the converted property (within the meaning of clause (ii) of section 1033 (a) (2) (E)) occurs during the 60-day period which ends on the day before the first day of the 12-month period, and

(3) such corporation elects the application of this subsection at such time and in such manner as the Secretary may by regulations prescribe, then for purposes of this

section such disposition shall be treated as a sale or exchange occurring within the 12: month period.

(f) Special Rule for LIFO Inventories. - In general, in the case of a corporation inventorying goods under the LIFO method, this section shall apply to gain from the sale or exchange of inventory assets only to the extent that such gain exceeds the LIFO recapture amount with respect to the assets.

(g) Title II or Similar Cases. - If a corporation completely liquidates pursuant to a plan of total liquidation adopted in a title II or similar case (within the meaning of section 368 (a) (3) (A)) --

> (1) for purposes of subsection (a) , the term "property" shall not include any item acquired on or after the date of the adoption of the liquidation plan if such item is not property within the meaning of subsection (b) (2), and

> (2) subsection (a) shall apply to sales and exchanges by the corporation of property within the period beginning on the date of the adoption of the liquidation plan and ending on the date of the termination of the case.] REPEALED

Sec. 337: This section has been revised and currently reads as follows:

NONRECOGNITION FOR PROPERTY DISTRIBUTED TO PARENT IN COMPLETE LIQUIDATION OF SUBSIDIARY.

(a) In General: No gain or loss shall be claimed by the liquidating corporation on the distribution to the 80-percent distributee of any property in a complete liquidation to which section 332 applies.

(b) Treatment of Indebtedness of Subsidiary, etc.
 (1) Indebtedness of subsidiary to parent: - If

> (A) a corporation is liquidated in a liquidation to which section 332 applies, and

> (B) on the date of the adoption of the liquidation plan, such corporation was indebted to the 80-percent distributee, for purposes of this section and section 336, any transfer of property to the 80-percent distributee in satisfaction of such indebtedness shall be treated as a distribution to such distributee in liquidation.

(2) Treatment of tax-exempt distributee:

    (A) In general: - Except as provided in subparagraph (B), paragraph (1) and subsection (a) shall not apply where the 80-percent distributee is an organization (other than a cooperative described in section 521) which is exempt from the tax imposed by this chapter.

    (B) Exception where property will be used in unrelated business: -
    (i) In general: - Subparagraph (A) shall not apply to any distribution of property to an organization described in section 511(a)(2) or 511(b)(2) if immediately after such distribution, such organization uses such property in an unrelated trade or business (as defined in section 513).

    (ii) Later disposition or change in use: - If any property to which clause (i) applied is disposed of by the organization acquiring such property, notwithstanding any other provision of law, any gain (not in excess of the amount not recognized by reason of clause (i) shall be included in such organization's unrelated business taxable income. For purposes of the preceding sentence, if such property ceases to be used in an unrelated trade or business of such organization, such organization shall be treated as having disposed of such property on the date of such cessation.

(c) 80-Percent Distributee: - For purposes of this section, the term "80-percent distributee" means only the organization which meets the 80-percent stock ownership requirements specified in section 332(b). For purposes of this section, the determination of whether any organization is an 80-percent distributee shall be made without regard to any regulation regarding consolidated return.

(d) Regulations: - The Secretary shall prescribe such regulations as are necessary or appropriate to ensure that the purposes of the amendments made to this subpart by the Tax Reform Act of 1986 include:
(1) regulations to ensure that such purposes may not be hindered through the use of any provision of law or regulations (including the consolidated return regulations and part III of this subchapter) and

(2) regulations providing for appropriate coordination of the provisions of this section with the provisions of this title relating to taxation of foreign corporations and their stockholders.

SEC. 341. COLLAPSIBLE CORPORATIONS.

(a) Treatment of Gain to Shareholders. -Gain from -

(1) the sale or exchange of stock of a collapsible corporation,
(2) a distribution -

(A) in total liquidation of a collapsible corporation if such distribution is treated under this part as in part or full payment in exchange for stock, or
(B) in partial liquidation (within the meaning of section 302(e) of a collapsible corporation if such distribution is treated under section 302(b) (4) as in partial or full payment in exchange for the stock, and

(3) a distribution made by a collapsible corporation which, under section 301 (c) (3) (A) , is treated, to the extent it exceeds the basis of the stock, in the same manner as a gain from property sold or exchanged, to the extent that it would be considered (but for the provisions of this section) as gain from the sale or exchange of a capital asset held for more than 1 year shall, except as otherwise provided in this section, be considered as ordinary income.

(b) Definitions.

(1) Collapsible corporation. -In this section, the term "collapsible corporation" refers to a corporation formed or availed of principally for the manufacture, construction, or production of property, for the purchase of property which (in the hands of the corporation) is property described in paragraph (3), or for the holding of stock in a corporation so formed or availed of, with a view to -

(A) the sale or exchange of stock by its shareholders (whether in liquidation or otherwise), or a distribution to its shareholders, before the realization by corporation manufacturing, constructing, producing, or purchasing the property of a substantial part of the taxable income to be derived from such property, and

(B) the realization by the shareholders of gain attributable to such property.

(2) Production or purchase of property. -For purposes of paragraph (1), a corporation shall be seemed to have manufactured, constructed, produced, or purchased property, if -

(A) it engaged in the construction, manufacture, or production of such property to any extent,

(B) it holds property having a basis determined, in part or in whole, by reference to the cost of such property in the hands of a person who manufactured, constructed, produced or purchased the property, or

(C) it holds property having a basis determined, in part or in whole, by reference to the cost of property manufactured, constructed, produced, or purchased by the corporation.

(3) Section 341 assets. - In this section, the term "section 341 assets" means property held for a period of less than 3 years which is -

(A) stock in trade of the corporation, or other property of a kind which would properly be included in the inventory of the corporation if on hand at the close of the taxable year;

(B) property held by the corporation mainly for sale to customers in the ordinary course of its trade or business;

(C) unrealized receivables or fees, except receivables from sales of property other than property described in this paragraph; or

(D) property described in section 1231(h) (without regard to any holding period therein provided), except for such property which is or has been used in connection with the construction, manufacture, production, or sale of property described in subparagraph (A) or (B)

In determining whether the 3-year holding period specified in this paragraph has been satisfied, section 333 shall apply, but no such period shall he deemed to begin before the completion of the construction, manufacture, production or purchase.

(4) Unrealized receivables. -For purposes of paragraph (3) (C), the term "unrealized receivables or fees" means, to the extent not previously inclusible in income under the method of accounting practised by the corporation, any rights (contractual or otherwise) to payment for

(A) goods delivered, or to be delivered, to the extent the proceeds therefrom would be treated as amounts received from the exchange or sale of property other than a capital asset, or

(B) services rendered or to be rendered.
(C) Presumption in Certain Cases. -

(1) In general. - In this section, a corporation shall, unless shown to the contrary, be deemed to be a collapsible corporation if (at the time of the sale or exchange, or the distribution, described in subsection (a) the fair market value of its section 341 assets (as defined in subsection (b) (3)) is

(A) 50 percent or more of the fair market value of its total assets, and

(B) 120 percent or more of the adjusted basis of such section 341 assets.

The absence of the conditions described in subparagraphs (A) and (B) shall not give rise to a presumption that the corporation was not a collapsible corporation.

(2) Determination of total assets. -In determining the fair market value of the total assets of a corporation for purposes of paragraph (1) (A) , there shall not he taken into account -

(A) cash,

(B) obligations which are capital assets in the hands of the corporation, and

(C) stock in any other corporation.

(d) Limitations on Application of Section. -In the case of gain realized by a shareholder with respect to his stock in a collapsible corporation, this section shall not apply -

(1) unless, at any time after the commencement of the construction, manufacture, or production of the property, or at the time of the purchase of the property described in subsection (b)(3) or at any time thereafter, such shareholder (A) owned (or was considered as owning) more than 5 percent in value of the outstanding stock of the corporation, or (B) owned stock which was considered as owned at such time by another shareholder who then owned (or was considered as owning) more than 50 percent in value of the outstanding stock of the corporation.

(2) to the gain recognized during a taxable year, unless more than 70 percent of such gain is attributable to the property so constructed, manufactured, produced, or purchased; and

(3) to gain realized after the expiration of 3 years following the completion of such construction, manufacture, production, or purchase.

For purposes of paragraph (1), the ownership of stock shall be determined in accordance with the rules prescribed in paragraphs (1) , (2) , (3) , (5) , and (6) of section 544 (a) (relating to personal holding companies) ; except that, in addition to the persons prescribed by paragraph (2) of that section, the family of an individual shall include the spouses of that individual's brothers and sisters (whether by the whole or half blood) and the spouses of that individual's lineal descendants.

(e)   Exceptions to Application of Section. -

(1) Sales or exchanges of stock. -For purposes of subsection (a) (1), a corporation shall not he considered to be a collapsible corporation with respect to any sale or exchange of stock of the corporation by a shareholder, if at the time of such sale or exchange, the sum of -

(A) the net unrealized appreciation in subsection (e) assets of the corporation (as defined in paragraph (5) (A)), plus

(B) if the shareholder owns more than 5% in value of the outstanding stock of the corporation.

SEC. 351. TRANSFER TO CORPORATION CONTROLLED BY TRANSFEROR.

(a)   General Rule. - Neither gain nor loss shall be recognized (a) General Rule. if property is transferred to a corporation by one or more persons solely in exchange for stock or securities in such corporation and immediately after the exchange such person or persons are in control (as defined in section 368 (c) of the corporation.

(b)   Receipt of Property. -If subsection (a) would apply to an exchange except for the fact that there is received, in addition to the stock or securities permitted to be received under subsection (a), other property or money, then -

(1) gain (if any) to such recipient shall be recognized, but not in excess of -

(A) the amount of money received, plus

(B) the fair market value of such other property received; and (2) no loss to such recipient shall be recognized.

(c) Special Rule. -In determining control, in this section, the fact that any corporate transferor distributes part or all of the stock which it receives in the exchange to its shareholders shall not be taken into account.

(d) [Services, Certain Indebtedness, and Accrued Interest Not Treated as Property

(1) services.

(2) indebtedness of the transferee corporation which is not evidenced by a security, or

(3) interest on indebtedness of the transferee corporation which accrued on or after the beginning of the transferor's holding period for the debt.] REPEALED

SEC. 362. BASIS TO CORPORATIONS.

(a) Property Acquired by Issuance of Stock or as Paid-in Surplus. -If property was acquired on or after June 22, , by a corporation -

(1) in connection with a transaction to which section 351 (relating to transfer of property to corporation controlled by transferor) applies, or

(2) as paid-in surplus or as a contribution to capital, then the basis will be the same as it would be in the hands of the transferor, increased in the amount of gain recognized to the transferor on such transfer. This subsection will not apply if the property acquired consists of securities or stock in a corporation a party to the reorganization, unless acquired by the exchange of stock or securities of the transferee (or of a corporation which is in control of the transferee) as the consideration in whole or in part for the transfer.

(b) Special Rule for Certain Contributions to Capital.

(1) Property other than money. - Notwithstanding subsection (a)(2), if property which is other than money

(A) is acquired by a corporation, on or after June 22, , as a contribution to capital, and

(B) is not contributed by a shareholder as such, then the basis of such property will be zero.

(2) Money. -Notwithstanding subsection (a) (2), if money

(A) is received by a corporation, on or after June 22, , as a contribution to capital, and

(B) is not contributed by a shareholder as such, then the basis of any property acquired with such money during the 12month period beginning on the day the contribution is received will be reduced by the amount of such a contribution. The excess (if any) of the amount of such a contribution over the amount of the reduction under the preceding sentence will be applied to the reduction (as of the last day of the period specified in the preceding sentence) of the basis of any other property held by the taxpayer. The particular properties to which the reductions required by this paragraph will be allocated will be determined under regulations prescribed by the Secretary.

SEC. 368. DEFINITIONS RELATING TO CORPORATE REORGANIZATIONS.

(a)   Reorganization.

(1) In general. -For purposes of parts I and II and this part, the term "reorganization" means -

(A) a consolidation or statutory merger;

(B) the acquisition by a corporation, in exchange solely for all or a part of its voting stock (or in exchange solely for all or a part of the voting stock of a corporation which is in control of the acquiring corporation), of stock of another corporation if, immediately after the acquisition the acquiring corporation had control immediately before the acquisition);

(C) the acquisition by a corporation, in exchange solely for all or a part of its voting stock (or in exchange solely for all or a part of the voting stock of a corporation which is in control of the acquiring corporation), of substantially all of the properties of another corporation, but in determining whether the exchange is solely for stock the assumption by the acquiring corporation of a liability of the other, or the fact that property acquired is subject to a liability, will be disregarded;

(D) a transfer by a corporation of part or all of its assets to another corporation if immediately after the transfer, or one or more of its shareholders including persons who were shareholders immediately before the transfer or any combination thereof, is in control of the corporation to which the assets are transferred; but only if, in pursuance of the plan, securities or stock of the corporation to which the assets are transferred are distributed in a transaction which qualifies under section 354, 355, or 356;

(E) a recapitalization;

(F) a mere change in form, identity, or place of organization of one corporation, however effected;
or

(G) a transfer by a corporation of part or all of its assets to another corporation in a title II or similar case; but only if, in pursuance of the plan, stock or securities of the corporation to which the assets are transferred are distributed in a transaction which qualifies under section 354, 355, or 356.

For acquisitions after December 31, 1988 or acquisitions in taxable years ending after such a date the amendment to SEC. 368 (a)(3)(D) must be reviewed which appears in SEC. 904 (a) of the Public Law 99-514, and which became effective as a result of the October 22, 1986 Tax Reform Act.

APPENDIX B

SEC SCHEDULE 14D-1, AND SCHEDULE 13G WITH INSTRUCTIONS

INSTRUCTIONS FOR COVER PAGE

(1) Names and Social security Numbers of Reporting Persons - Furnish the full legal name of each person for whom the report is filed - i.e., each person required to sign the schedule itself - including each member of a group. Do not include the name of a person required to be identified in the report but who is not a reporting person. Reporting persons are also requested to furnish their Social Security or I.R.S. identification numbers, although disclosure of such numbers is voluntary, not mandatory (see "SPECIAL INSTRUCTIONS FOR COMPLYING WITH SCHEDULE 14D-1", below).

(2) If any of the shares beneficially owned by a reporting person are held as a member of a group and such membership is expressly affirmed, please check row 2(a). If the membership in a group is disclaimed or the reporting person describes a relationship with other persons but does not affirm the existence of a group, please cheek row 2(b) (unless a joint filing pursuant to Rule 13d-1(f) (1) in which case it may not be necessary to check row 2 (b).

(3) The third row is for SEC internal use, please leave blank.

(4) Source of Funds - Classify the source of funds or other consideration to be used in making purchases as required to be disclosed pursuant to Item 4 of the schedule and insert the appropriate symbol (or symbols if more than one is necessary) in row (4):

Category of Source	Symbol
Subject Company (company whose securities are being acquired)	SC
Bank	BK
Affiliate (of reporting person)	AF
Working Capital (of reporting person)	WC
Personal Funds (of reporting person)	PF
Other	OO

(5) If disclosure of legal proceedings or actions is required pursuant to either Items 2(e) or 2(f) of Schedule 14d-1, row 5 should be checked.

(6) **Citizenship or Place of Organization** - Furnish citizenship if the named reporting person is a natural person. Otherwise, furnish the place of organization. (See Item 2 of Schedule 14D-1.)

(7),(9) Aggregate Amount Beneficially Owned by Each Reporting Person, etc. - Rows (7) and (9) are to be completed in accordance with the Instructions to Item 6 of Schedule 14D-1. All percentages are to be rounded off to nearest tenth (one place after decimal point).

(8) Check if the aggregate amount reported as beneficially owned in row (7) does not include shares as to which beneficial ownership is disclaimed.

(10) Type of Reporting Person - Please classify each "reporting person" according to the following breakdown and place the appropriate symbol (or symbols, i.e., if more than one is applicable, insert all applicable symbols) on the form:

Category	Symbol
Broker Dealer	BD
Bank	BK
Insurance Company	IC
Investment Company	N
Investment Adviser	IA
Employee Benefit Plan, Pension Fund, or Endowment Fund	EP
Parent Holding Company	HC
Group Member	GM
Corporation	CO
Partnership	PN
Individual	IN
Other	00

NOTES:

Attach as many copies of the second part of the cover page as are needed, one reporting person per page.

Filing persons may, in order to avoid unnecessary duplication, answer items on the schedules (Schedule 13D, 13G or 14D-1) by appropriate cross references to an item or items on the cover page(s). This approach may he used only where the cover page item or items provide all the disclosure required by the schedule item. Moreover, such a use of a cover page item will result in the item becoming a part of the schedule and accordingly being considered as "filed" for purposes of Section 18 of the Securities Exchange Act or otherwise subject to the liabilities of that section of the Act.

Reporting persons may comply with their cover page filing requirements by filing either completed copies of the blank forms available from the Commission, printed or typed facsimiles, or computer-printed facsimiles, provided the documents filed have identical formats to the forms prescribed in the Commission's regulations and meet existing Securities Exchange Act rules as to such matters as clarity and size (Securities Exchange Act Rule 12b-12).

SECURITIES AND EXCHANGE COMMISSION
Washington, D.C. 20549

SCHEDULE 14D-1

Tender Offer Statement Pursuant to Section 14 (d) (1) of the Securities Exchange Act of 1934
(Amendment No. (_))*

(Name of Subject Company)

(Bidder)

(Title of Class of Securities)

(CUSIP Number of Class of Securities)

(Name, Address, and Telephone Numbers of Person Authorized to Receive Notices and Communications on Behalf of Bidder)

NOTE: The remainder of this cover page is only to be completed if this Schedule 14D-1 (or amendment thereto) is being filed, inter alia, to satisfy the reporting requirements of section 13(d) of the Securities Exchange Act of 1934. See General Instructions D, E and F to Schedule 14D-1.

*The remainder of this cover page shall be filled out for a reporting person's initial filing on this form with respect to the subject class of securities, and for any subsequent amendment containing information which would alter the disclosure provided in a prior cover page.

The information required in the remainder of this cover page shall not be deemed to be "filed" for the purpose of Section 18 of the Securities Exchange Act 1934 ("Act") or otherwise subject to the liabilities of that section of the Act but shall be subject to all other provisions of the Act (however, see the Notes).

(Continued on following page(s))

Page 1 of (_____) Pages

CUSIP No._____   Page_____of_____Pages

14D-1

1	Name of Reporting Person_____ S.S. or I.R.S. Identification No. of Above Person_____	
2	Check the Appropriate row if a Member of a Group* (a)_____ (b)_____	
3	SEC Use Only_____	
4	Sources of Funds*_____	
5	Check if Disclosure of Legal Proceedings is Required Pursuant to Items 2(e) or 2(f) _____	
6	Citizenship or Place of Organization_____	
7	Aggregate Amount Beneficially Owned by Each Reporting Person_____	
8	Check if the Aggregate Amount in Row (7) Excludes Certain Shares* _____	
9	Percent of Class Represented by Amount in Row (7)_____	
10	Type of Reporting Person*_____	

*SEE INSTRUCTIONS BEFORE FILLING OUT!

INSTRUCTIONS FOR COVER PAGE

(1) **Names and Social Security Numbers of Reporting Persons -**

Furnish the full legal name of each person for whom the report is filed -i.e., each person required to sign the schedule itself - including each member of a group. Do not include the name of a person required to be identified in the report but who is not a reporting person. Reporting persons are also requested to furnish their Social Security or I.R.S. identification numbers, although disclosure of such numbers is voluntary, not mandatory (see "SPECIAL INSTRUCTIONS FOR COMPLYING WITH SCHEDULE, 13G," below).

(2) If any of the shares beneficially owned by a reporting person are held as a member of a group and such membership is expressly affirmed, please check row 2 (a). If the membership in a group is disclaimed or the reporting person describes a relationship with other persons but does not affirm the existence of a group, please check row 2(b) (unless a joint filing pursuant to Rule 13D - 1(F) 1 in which case it may not be necessary to check row 2 (b)).

(3) The third row is for SEC internal use; please leave blank.

(4) **Citizenship or Place of Organization -** Furnish citizenship if the named reporting person is a natural person. Otherwise, furnish place of organization.

(5)-(9),(11) **Aggregate Amount Beneficially Owned by EACH Reporting Person,** etc. - Rows (5) through (9) inclusive, and (11) are to be completed in accordance with the provisions of Item 4 of Schedule 13G. All percentages are to be rounded off to the nearest tenth (one place after decimal point).

(10) Check if the aggregate amount reported as beneficially owned in row (9) does not included shares as to which beneficial ownership is disclaimed pursuant to Rule 13d-4 (17 CFR 240.13d-4) under the Securities Exchange Act of 1934.

(12) **Type of Reporting Person -** Please classify each "reporting person" according to the following breakdown (see Item 3 of schedule 13G) and place the appropriate symbol on the form:

Category	Symbol
Broker Dealer	BD
Bank	BK
Insurance Company	IC

Investment Company	N
Investment Adviser	IA
Employee Benefit Plan, Pension Fund, or Endowment Fund	EP
Parent Holding Company	HC
Corporation	CO
Partnership	PN
Individual	IN
Other	OO

NOTES:

Attach as many copies of the second Part of the cover page as are needed, one reporting person per page.

Filing persons may, in order to avoid unnecessary duplication, answer items on the schedules (Schedule 13D, 13G or 14D-1) by appropriate cross references to an item or items on the cover page(s). This approach may only be used where the cover page item or items provide all the disclosure required by the schedule item. Moreover, such a use of a cover pace item will result in the item becoming a part of the schedule and accordingly being considered as "filed" for purposes of Section 18 of the Securities Exchange Act or otherwise subject to the liabilities of that section of the Act.

Reporting Persons may comply with their cover page filing requirements by filing either completed copies of the blank forms available from the Commission, printed or typed facsimiles, or computer printed facsimiles, provided the documents filed have identical formats to the forms prescribed in the Commission's regulations and meet existing Securities Exchange Act rules as to such matters as clarity and size (Securities Exchange Act Rule 12b-12) .

SPECIAL INSTRUCTIONS FOR COMPLYING WITH SCHEDULE 13G

Under Section 13 (d) , 13 (g) and 23 of the Securities Exchange Act of 1934 and the rules and regulations thereunder, the commission is authorized to solicit the information required to he supplied by this schedule by certain security holders of certain issuers.

Disclosure of the information specified in this schedule is mandatory, except for Social Security or I.R.S. identification numbers, disclosure of which is voluntary. The information will be used for the primary purpose of determining and disclosing the holdings of certain beneficial owners of certain equity securities. This statement will be made a matter of public record. Therefore, any information given will be available for inspection by any member of the public.

Because of the public nature of the information, the Commission can utilize it for a variety of purposes, including referral to other governmental authorities or securities self-regulatory organizations for investigatory purposes or in connection with litigation involving the Federal securities laws or other civil, criminal or regulatory statutes or provisions. Social Security or I.R.S. identification numbers, if furnished, will assist the Commission in identifying security holders and, therefore, in promptly processing statements of beneficial ownership of securities.

Failure to disclose the information requested by this schedule, except for Social Security or I.R.S. identification numbers, may result in civil or criminal action against the persons involved for violation of the Federal securities laws and rules promulgated thereunder.

SECURITIES AND EXCHANGE COMMISSION
Washington, D.C. 20549

SCHEDULE 13G

Under the Securities Exchange Act of 1934
(Amendment No. (_____)*

_____

(Name of Issuer)

_____

(Title of Class of Securities)

_____

(CUSIP Number)

Check the following box if a fee is being paid with this statement. (A fee is not required only if the filing person: (1) has a previous statement on file reporting beneficial ownership of more than five percent of the class of securities described in Item 1; and (2) has filed no amendment subsequent thereto reporting beneficial ownership of five percent or less of such class.) (See Rule 13d-7.)

*The remainder of this cover page shall be filled out for a reporting person's initial filing on this form with respect to the subject class of securities, and for any subsequent amendment containing information which would alter the disclosures provided in a prior cover page.

The information required in the remainder of this cover page shall not be deemed to be "filed" for the purpose of Section 18 of the Securities Exchange Act of 1934 ("Act") or otherwise subject to the liabilities of that section of the Act but shall be subject to all other provisions of the Act (however, see the Notes).

(Continued on following page(s))

Page 1 of (_____) Pages

CUSIP No._____ Page____ _of____ Pages

13G

1 Name of Reporting Person_____
   S.S. or I.R.S. Identification No. of Above Person_____

2 Check where Appropriate if a Member of a Group*   (a)_____

                                                            (b)_____

3 SEC Use Only_____

4 Citizenship or Place of Organization_____

Number of Shares_____   5   Sole Voting Power Shares_____

Beneficially Owned By_____   6   Shared Voting Power_____

Each Reporting_____   7   Sole Dispositive Power_____

Person With_____ 8   Shared Dispositive Power_____

9 Aggregate Amount Beneficially Owned by Each Reporting Person_____

10 Check if the Aggregate Amount in Row (9) Excludes Certain Shares*   _____

11 Percent of Class Represented by Amount in Row (9)_____

12 Type of Reporting Person*_____

SEC 1745(6-80)   *SEE INSTRUCTIONS BEFORE FILLING OUT!

APPENDIX C

SEC SCHEDULE 13D WITH INSTRUCTIONS ALONG WITH PAGE 3 THROUGH PAGE 5 OF THE BENDIX SEC SUBMISSION

INSTRUCTIONS FOR COVER PAGE

(1) Names and Social Security Numbers of Reporting Persons

Furnish the full legal name of each person for whom the report is filed - i.e., each person required to sign the schedule itself -- including each member of a group. Do not include the name of a person required to be identified in the report but who is not a reporting person. Reporting persons are also requested to furnish their Social Security or I.R.S. identification numbers, although disclosure of such numbers is voluntary, not mandatory (see "SPECIAL INSTRUCTIONS FOR COMPLYING WITH SCHEDULE 13-D," below).

(2) If any of the shares beneficially owned by a reporting person are held as a member of a group and such membership is expressly affirmed, please check row 2(a). If the membership in a group is disclaimed or the reporting person describes a relationship with other persons but does not affirm the existence of a group, please check row 2(b) (unless a joint filing pursuant to Rule 13d-l(f) (1) in which case it may not he necessary to check row 2 (b)).

(3) The Third row is for SEC internal use; please leave blank.

(4) Classify the source of funds or other consideration used or to be used in making the purchases as required to be disclosed pursuant to Item 3 of Schedule 13D and insert the appropriate symbol (or symbols if more than one is necessary) in row (4):

Category of Source	Symbol
Subject Company (Company whose securities are being acquired)	SC
Bank	BK
Affiliate (of reporting person)	AF
Working Capital (of reporting person)	WC
Personal Funds (of reporting person)	PF
Other	00

(5) If disclosure of legal proceedings or actions is required pursuant to either Items 2 (d) or 2 (e) of Schedule 13D, row 5 should be checked.

(6) **Citizenship or Place of Organization** - Furnish citizenship if the named reporting person is a natural person. Otherwise, furnish place of organization. (See Item 2 of Schedule 13D).

(7)-(11) **Aggregate Amount Beneficially Owned by Each Reporting Person, etc.** - Rows (7) through (11), inclusive, and (13) are to be completed in accordance with the provisions of Item 5 of Schedule 13D. All percentages are to be rounded off to nearest tenth (one place after decimal point).

(12) Check if the aggregate amount reported as beneficially owned in row (11) does not include shares which the reporting person discloses in the report but as to which beneficial ownership is disclaimed pursuant to Rule 13d-4 (17 CFR 240.13(d-4) under the Securities Exchange Act of 1934.

(14) **Type of Reporting Person** - Please classify each "reporting person" according to the following breakdown and place the appropriate symbol (or symbols, i.e., if more than one is applicable, insert all applicable symbols) on the form:

Category	Symbol
Broker Dealer	BD
Bank	BK
Insurance Company	IC
Investment Company	IV
Investment Adviser	IA
Employee Benefit Plan, Pension Fund, Endowment Fund	EP
Parent Holding Company	HC
Corporation	CO
Partnership	PN
Individual	IN
Other	00

NOTES:

Attach as many copies of the second part of the cover page as are needed, one reporting person per page.

Filing persons may, in order to avoid unnecessary duplication, answer items on the schedules (schedule 13D, 13G, or 14D-1) by appropriate cross references to an item or items on the cover page (s) . This approach may only be used where the cover page item or items provide all the disclosure required by the schedule item. Moreover, such a use of a cover page item will result in the item becoming part of the schedule and accordingly being considered as "filed" for purposes of Section 18 of the Securities Exchange Act or otherwise subject to the liabilities of that section of the Act.

Reporting persons may comply with their cover page filing requirements by filing either completed copies of the blank forms available from the Commission, printed or typed facsimiles, or computer printed facsimiles, provided the documents filed have identical formats to the forms prescribed in the Commission's regulations and meet existing Securities Exchange Act rules as to such matters as clarity and size (Securities Exchange Act Rule 12b-12).

SPECIAL INSTRUCTIONS FOR COMPLYING WITH SCHEDULE, 13D

Under Sections 13 (d) and 23 of the Securities Exchange Act of 1934 and the rules and regulations thereunder, the Commission is authorized to solicit the information required to be supplied by this schedule by certain security holders of certain issuers.

Disclosure of the information specified in this schedule is mandatory, except for Social Security or I.R.S. identification numbers, disclosure of which is voluntary. The information will he used for the primary purpose of determining and disclosing the holdings of certain beneficial owners of certain equity securities. This statement will he made a matter of public record. Therefore, any information given will be available for inspection by any member of the public.

Because of the public nature of the information, the Commission can utilize it for a variety of purposes, including referral to other governmental authorities or securities self-regulatory organizations for investigatory purposes or in connection with litigation involving the Federal securities laws or other civil, criminal or regulatory statements or provisions. Social Security or I.R.S. identification numbers, if furnished, will assist the Commission in identifying security holders and, therefore, in promptly processing statements of beneficial ownership of securities.

Failure to disclose the information requested by this schedule, except for Social Security or I.R.S. identification numbers, may result in civil or criminal action against the persons involved for violation of the Federal securities laws and rules promulgated thereunder.

APPENDICES

SECURITIES AND EXCHANGE, COMMISSION
Washington, D.C. 20949

SCHEDULE 13D

Under the Securities Exchange Act of 1934
(Amendment No. (_))

_____\
(Name of Issuer)

_____\
(CUSIP Number)

_____\
(Name, Address and Telephone Number of Person Authorized to Receive Notices and Communications)

_____\
(Date of Event which Requires Filing of this Statement)

If the filing person has previously filed a statement on schedule 13G to report the acquisition which is the subject of this Schedule 13D, and is filing this schedule because of Rule 13d-1(b) (3) or (4), check the following box ☐.

Check the following box if a fee is being paid with the statement ☐. (A fee is not required only if the reporting person: (1) has a previous statement on file reporting beneficial ownership of more than five percent of the class of securities described in Item 1; and (2) has filed no amendment subsequent thereto reporting beneficial ownership of five percent or less of such class.) (See Rule 13d-7.)

Note: Six copies of this statement, including all exhibits, should he filed with the Commission. See Rule 13-d-l(a) for other parties to whom copies are to be sent.

*The remainder of this cover page shall he filed for a reporting person's initial filing on this form with respect to the subject class of securities, and for any subsequent amendment containing information which would alter disclosures provided in a prior cover page.

The information required on the remainder of this cover page shall not be deemed to be "filed" for the purpose of Section 18 of the Securities Exchange Act of 1934 ("Act") or otherwise subject to the liabilities of that section of the Act but shall be subject to all other provisions of the Act (however, see the Notes).

(Continued on following page (s))
Page 1 of_____Pages

CUSIP No._____ Page____ _of____ Pages

13D

1 Name of Reporting Person
S.S. or I.R.S. Identification No. of Above Person_____

2 Check Where Appropriate if a Member of a Group* (a) _____
                                                    (b) _____

3 SEC Use Only_____

4 Source of Funds_____

5 Check if disclosure of legal proceedings is required pursuant
  to items 2 (d) or 2(o)_____

6 Citizenship or Place of Organization_____

Number of   7 Sole Voting Power _____
    Shares_____

Beneficially   8 Shared Voting Power_____
   Owned By_____

Each   9 Sole Dispositive Power_____
    Reporting_____
Person   10 Shared Dispositive Power_____
    With_____

11 Aggregate Amount Beneficially Owned by Each Reporting Person_____

12 Check if the Aggregate Amount in Row (11) Excludes Certain Shares* _____

13 Percent of Class Represented by Amount in Row (11)_____

14 Type of Reporting Person*_____

SEC 1746(6-00)   *SEE INSTRUCTIONS BEFORE FILLING OUT!

BENDIX CORPORATE SUPPLEMENT OF SCHEDULE 13D

This Amendment No. I amends the Statement on Schedule 13D (which was deemed to be filed upon filing of the Final Amendment to the Statement on Schedule 14D-1 dated September 30, 1982) of The Bendix Corporation ("Bendix") relating to the Common Stock, par value $1.00 per share (the "Shares"), of Martin Marietta Corporation ("Martin Marietta"), as follows:

Item 2. Identity and Background.

Appendix I hereto, which is incorporated herein by reference, sets forth, with respect to each director and executive officer of Bendix, the following information: (a) name and business address; (b) present principal occupation or employment and the name and principal business, and address (which is the same as that referred to under (a)), of any corporation or other organization in which such employment is conducted; and (c) citizenship.

Item 4. Purpose of Transaction.

See Item 5 below.

Item 5. Interest in Securities of the Issuer.

On December 21, 1982, Bendix sold 100 shares of Common Stock, par value $1.00 per share, of Bendix Acquisition Corporation, a Delaware corporation ("BAC"), representing all of the outstanding capital stock of BAC, to Allied Corporation, a New York corporation ("Allied"), in exchange for 1000 shares of Adjustable Rate Series E Cumulative Preferred Shares of Allied having a stated and an initial value equivalent to $1,193,674,470. Such sale was made pursuant to the terms of a Stock Purchase Agreement, dated as of September 24, 1982, as amended as of November 12, 1982 and as of December 6, 1982, among Bendix, BAC, Allied, Martin Marietta and ML Holding Corp. (the "Stock Purchase Agreement"). A copy of the Stock Purchase Agreement is attached hereto as Exhibit 1 and is incorporated herein by reference. At the time of such sale, the assets of BAC included 25,582,500 Shares (approximately 70% of the Shares on a fully diluted basis), representing all of the Shares beneficially owned by Bendix as of December 21, 1982. Accordingly, Bendix no longer beneficially owns any Shares.

Item 6. Contracts, Arrangements, Understandings or Relationships with Respect to Securities of the Issuer.

Reference is made to Exhibit 1, attached hereto and incorporated herein by reference.

Item 7. Material to be Filed as Exhibits.

Exhibit 1: Stock Purchase Agreement, dated as of September 24, 1982, as amended as of November 12, 1982 and as of December 6, 1982

SIGNATURE

After reasonable inquiry and to the best of its knowledge and belief, the undersigned certifies that the information set forth in this statement is true, complete and correct.

Date:_____

THE BENDIX CORPORATION

By_____

GLOSSARY

A Accounts receivable (1) A current asset showing claims against customers for services rendered or goods sold on account.

Acquisition (2) An acquisition is the act of buying a stock or an asset. See Stock Acquisition and Asset Acquisition.

Amortization (3) A gradual depletion of an account balance to reflect the allocation of premiums to time periods by charges to the income statement.

Annuity (4) A series of payments or receipts of a fixed amount at fixed intervals for a specified number of periods.

Arbitrage (5) A buying of securities in one market and selling them at a higher price in another market.

Asset (6) All entries on a balance sheet that reflect the entire resources of a person, organization or business such as cash, accounts receivable, inventory, land, building, equipment patents and goodwill.

Asset Acquisition (7) A buyer acquires all or part of the assets of the seller after the approval of the seller's stockholders.

B Bankruptcy (1) A legal process by which a business is liquidated under the jurisdiction of the courts of law.

Balance Sheet (2) The financial statement of an organization or business disclosing assets, liabilities and capital equities as of a specific date.

Break-even Analysis (3) A technique used in studying the functional relationship among total fixed cost, total variable cost, and profits.

Blue-Sky Laws (4) State laws that regulate the acquisition or sale of securities.

Bond (5) A negotiable long-term debt instrument. For further explanation, see "debenture" and "indenture."

Book Value (6) The amount at which assets or liabilities are recorded on the firm's books.

Buyer (7) An individual or a corporation who acquires the assets or shares of another entity.

C

Call Premium (1) The amount in excess over the face value that a corporation should pay when it elects to call a security.

Capital Asset (2) Any asset with a life greater than one year that is bought or sold in the ordinary course of a business operation.

Capital Structure (3) The composition of long-term financing of a corporation represented by the mix of long-term debt, preferred stock and net worth.

Cash Budget (4) A schedule showing cash receipts and disbursements within a firm over a specific period of time. The objective is to show the net cash from operation and the beginning and ending cash balance and to avoid cash shortage.

Cash Flow From Operation (5) This shows all cash receipts and cash disbursements for a specific period. Excess receipts over disbursements is an inflow while excess disbursements over receipts is an outflow.

Consolidation (6) This involves the combination of two or more companies with a new entity being formed. The new entity (corporation) absorbs all the assets while the individual companies in the consolidation would cease to exist under their former identity.

Cost of Capital (7) The discount or interest rate that should be used in the evaluation of an investment.

Controlled Company (8) A company that has the major part or all of its common voting stock held by another corporation.

D

Debenture (1) A long-term bond that is not secured by a mortgage or a prior claim against a specific property.

Debt (2) An amount of money owed by a corporation or individual that is not executory.

Debt Financing (3) Arranging to raise funds through debt in order to finance a corporate expansion and/or acquisition.

Debt Ratio (4) Total debt divided by total assets.

Depreciation (5) The amortization of fixed assets in order to allocate the asset cost over its useful life. (See Straight-line, Double-declining, and Sum-of-the-years digits.)

Disclosure (6) The process of making financial and managerial information available about a corporation or any business entity.

Divestment (7) The process of eliminating a portion of a line of business or the firm as a whole and using the freed resources for some other purpose.

Divestiture (8) See divestment.

Double-declining (9) A method of depreciation equal to a fixed percentage which is equivalent to twice the straight percentage.

E

ESOP (1) Employee stock ownership plans offer employees shares of company stock as a benefit.

$ Earnings Multiplier (2) A multiplier used to determine the market price per share of a firm's common stock. It is the same as price earning ratio (P/E) which is the ratio of price to earnings.

Earnings Per Share (EPS) (3) Income per share available to common stockholders (net income less preferred stock dividends divided by the average number of common shares outstanding).

Equity (4) The net worth of a corporation/firm encompassing capital stock, capital surplus and retained earnings.

Equity Financing (5) The sale of preferred and/or common stock to raise funds for acquisition of additional firm/product line or expansion of an existing operation.

Exchange Rate (6) A rate at which one country's currency can he exchanged for another.

F

Fiduciary Duties (1) Involves the performance of members of the board of directors of a company in a manner that serves the best interest of the stockholders, who they ultimately represent, in any takeover attempt or merger.

FIFO (2) An inventory method known as first-in, first-out. It assumes that earlier costs apply to goods sold and most recent costs apply to the balance of goods on hand.

Fixed assets (3) An accounting term used for land, building, equipment, furniture and fixtures.

Fixed Charges (4) Charges that do not vary with the level of production.

Flip-in Poison Pill (5) A flip-in strategy allows the current shareholders to acquire more shares of the company at a discount.

Flip-over Poison Pill (6) A flip-over strategy allows the shareholders of the target company to acquire shares of the acquirer at a discount subsequent to the merger.

Float (4) A term used to refer to the time interval between the date a person or business entity writes a check to the date on which the funds are drawn.

G

Greenmail (1) A payment made by a target corporation to a corporate raider for a block of its stock that is owned by the raider who threatens and plans a hostile take-over of the target corporation.

Golden Parachutes (2) A form of bonus compensation given to a selected group of a company's top management in order to retain them by giving them guaranteed compensation in case the acquirer decides to fire them or retire them subsequent to the takeover/merger.

Goodwill (3) The excess of the cost of a going concern over its book value.

I

Indenture (1) An agreement drawn up between the issuer of a bond and the bondholders, giving the bondholders or their representative the right to periodically review the financial records of the issuer of the bond.

Internal Rate of Return (IRR) (2) The rate of return which, when used to discount the future cash flow from an investment, would equate the future discounted value with that of the initial cost of the investment.

L

Leveraged Buy Out (LBO) (1) An LBO is a financial technique to purchase a company using borrowed money with the hope of liquidating a part and paying some of the debt incurred in the process.

LIFO (2) Last-in, first-out. An inventory method which assumes that the most recent costs apply to the goods sold while the earliest costs apply to the balance of goods on hand.

Line of Credit (3) A financial agreement between a financial institution and a business firm whereby the financial institution commits itself to lend the business firm a specified amount of money for a certain period of time, usually equal to or less than one year.

Liquidation (4) The term covers the sale of non-cash assets and the settlement of all liabilities and the distribution of the remaining cash to stockholders (owners).

Lock-up Option (5) A method used to discourage an acquirer from further pursuing a company. In this case the target company discourages the acquirer by negotiating the sale of certain assets or a golden jewel division to a third entity.

M   Merger (1) The combination of two firms into a single entity.

Minority Interest (2) Refers to ownership of shares in a controlled company.

N   Net Present Value (NPV) (1) The NPV is equal to the present value of future cash flows discounted at the cost of capital or opportunity cost less the present value of the investment cost.

Net worth (2) See Equity.

P   Pac Man Defense (3) An aggressive approach that the target company utilizes in trying to takeover the acquirer by making a counter tender offer to the acquirer's shareholders.

Parking (4) Is an offensive tactics used by raiders in a takeover of a company.

Poison Pill (5) An anti-takeover approach that a target company may adopt to discourage a raider or a hostile acquirer from pursuing a takeover. An example of a poison pill may be the introduction of convertible preferred stock.

Pooling of Interest (6) An accounting method that combines the book values of assets and equities of the separate firms to form the balance sheet of the surviving firm. Under this type of method, no goodwill is recorded. As of June 2001 this method was repealed by the intoduction of FAS 141.

Portfolio (7) A combination of assets and/or securities to minimize risk through diversification.

Present Value (8) The value today of payments to be received in the future.
Price/Earnings Ratio (P/E) (4) See Earnings Multiplier.

Prime Rate (10) The rate of interest major lending banks charge other banks or borrowers with high credit ratings.

Pro Forma (11) Projected financial statement based on specific assumptions.

Proxy (12) A statement signed by a stockholder of a company giving management the authority to vote on its behalf.

Purchase Method (13) An accounting method for business combinations that allows a corporation to record goodwill equal to that of the excess of the paid price for a firm over the book value of the acquired firm.

R

Reinvestment (1) The process by which cash flows received from sale or liquidation of an investment are reinvested.

Repatriation of Funds (2) The process of transfer of funds from an overseas subsidiary's profit to the parent company headquarters.

Reorganization (3) The process by which a financially troubled company can restate its assets at current market value and reduce its financial structure to reflect that reduction in assets.

Retained Earnings (4) The sum of net income that is not paid out in dividends.

Return On Investment (ROI) (5) The net profit from an investment for a period divided by the average investment during the period.

$$ROI = \frac{\text{Net Profit After Tax}}{\text{Sales}} \times \frac{\text{Sales}}{\text{Avg. Investment}} = \frac{\text{Net Profit After Tax}}{\text{Avg. Investment}}$$

S

Sarbanes-Oxley Act (1) This law was enacted in July 2002 and signed by President George W. Bush. It deals with reporting of companies' financial statements and holds the Chief Executive Officer and the Chief Financial Officer of a publicly held company responsible for certifying the financial reports released to the shareholders.

Shark Repellant (2) Are provisions that are incorporated into the corporate charter with the purpose of discouraging unwanted acquirers. These provisions may include a staggered board of directors or the requirement of a fair price etc.

Salvage Value (3) The value of a depreciated asset at the end of a specific period.

Seller (4) A corporation, partnership, or sole proprietorship in the market for selling a business entity.

Sinking Fund (5) A fund set aside for the retirement of long-term debt.

Spin-Off (6) A spin-off involves the transfer of assets to a newly formed subsidiary in exchange for the subsidiary's outstanding common stock and then distributing this common stock to the stockholders of the parent company.

Split-Off (7) A split-off involves the transfer of a portion of the assets or a segment of the main corporation, such as a division or a product combination, to the existing stockholders who will surrender their stock in the main corporation for the assets they are receiving.

Split-Up (8) In this case a main corporation is split into two subsidiaries and the assets and corresponding liabilities from the main corporation are transferred to these subsidiaries. The sharehholders of the main corporation surrender their shares for the stock in any of the two newly formed entities. The main company is then liquidated and its stock ceases to exist.

Stock (9) Shares in a corporation representing claims against assets after payment of creditors. It is usually preferred and common or common shares only.

Stockholders (10) Owners of shares of a corporation.

T   Take-over (1) An offer made directly to the shareholders of a company by another corporation without prior consent of top management of the target company. Usually the purchase price per share offered is higher than the market value of the stock.

Tender-offer (2) An offer to buy the shares of a corporation at a stated price per share. The offer is either made to management of the target corporation or directly to the stockholders.

Trustee (3) A selected representative of bondholders who works in their best interest and represents them in all communication with the corporation/organization issuing the bond.

U   Underwriter (1) A corporation or individual who underwrites securities issue by insuring the risk of unfavorable market prices.

V   Vertical Integration (1) Vetical integration occurs when a company acquires its supplier or its distributor.

W   Warrant (1) An option to purchase a stated number of common stock for a specified price.

White Knight (2) A friendly acquirer who is sought by management to save the target company from a hostile takeover attempt. The White Knight is a more compatible and favorable merger partner in that it often allows imcumbent management to remain in place.

Working Capital (3) A business investment in cash, marketable securities, account receivables, and inventories. The gross working capital is equal to current assets while the net working capital is equal to current assets less current liabilities.

INDEX

A

Accounting records,
    investigation of, 67-73
    See also "Pooling of interest"
    See also "Purchase method"
Accounts Receivable, G`
Acquirer, 12, G
Acquirer, goals of, 8-9, 12-13, 22, 54
Acquisition, financial analysis, 28-29
Acquisition, financing of, 63
Acquisition, types, 7-8
Acquisition candidate, review of, 21, 53-55
Acquisition contract, 79-83
    checklist, 80
    closing process, 83
    factors, 80
    functions, 81
    organized pattern, 81-83
Acquisition method, 29-30
Acquisition price, determination, 28-29, 57-58
Acquisition procedure, 22, 55-57, 68-73
Acquisition objectives, 8-9, 54-55
Amortization, G
Annuity, G
Anti-trust law, 46, 76-77
Asset, G
Asset, acquisition, 7, 49, G
Asset turnover, ATO, 89-90, 92
Asset value, 29-31, 57, 100

B

Balance sheet, G
Bankruptcy, 37-38, 81, 122, G
Blue-sky laws, 43-47, G
Bond, G
Book value, 57, 61, G
Break-even analysis, G
Buyer, 8-9, G
Buyer's objectives, 21-22, 54
    Buyer's screening criteria, 56

C

Call premium, G
Capital asset, G

Capital structure, G
Capitalization of retained earnings, 78
Cash budget, G
Cash flow, G
Clayton Act, 16, 44, 72
Closing costs, 98-100, 115
Comparative price analysis of an acquisition, 29
Conglomerate corporate growth, 6
Consolidation, 8, G
Controlled company, G
Corporate growth, types, 5-8
Corporate long-range plan, 24, 41, 54
Corporate reorganization, 12
Corporate strategy, 5-6, 39
Cost of capital, G
Currency exchange, 78

D

Debenture, G
Debt, 63, G
Debt financing, 63, G
Debt ratio, 90, 92, G
De Facto merger, 8
Deployment of resources, rationalization, 39
Depreciation methods, 29, G
Disclosure of information, 44, G
Discounted cash flow, DCF, 89
Diversification strategy, 6, 54
Divestiture, G
Divestment, definition of, 9, 36-42, G
Divestment, effects of, 10
Divestment for Profit, 36
Divestment, involuntary, 37-38
Divestment, objectives of, 9-10, 12, 38, 88
Divestment, types, 9, 37
Divestment, voluntary, 37
Divestment alternatives, 96-97, 101-102, 107
Divestment analysis, 97
Divestment candidates
    financial evaluation, 88-89
    ranking of, 91-93
    selection methods, 40-41
Divestment plan, 87-88
Double declining, G

---
* G Locate word in Glossary

E

Earning per share, EPS, 23, 29-31, 33, 54-55, 89, 91, 97, 100, 112-114, G
Earnings multiplier, G
Equity, 33, 59, 64, G
Equity financing, 63, G
Exchange rate, G
Exemption of FTC notification filing, 16-17
Exemption of SEC notification filing, 16-17
European Economic Community, EEC, 76-77

F

Fair market value, 57-58, 62-63
Federal Securities Laws, 14
Federal Trade Commission, FTC, 10, 16-17
FIFO, 31, 100, G
Filing qualifications, 48-49
Filing requirements, 17-18, 44, 48-49
Financial analysis, 28-20, 31-33
Financial projections, 112
Fixed assets, G
Flip-in Poison Pill, G
Float, G
Foreign country restrictions, 77-78

G

Generally accepted accounting principles (GAAP) 32, 69
Geographical segmentation, 23
Greenmail, G
Goodwill, 30, G

H

Hart-Scott-Rodino Act, 47
Horizontal corporate growth, 4, 6-7, 56
Horizontal integration, 5-6, 56

I

Indentures, G
Internal Rate of Return, IRR, 40, 89, 92-93, G
Internal Revenue Code, IRC, 12-13, 102, 104-105
Inventory methods, 31
Inventory policies, 31`
Investigating acquisition candidates, 69-73
Investment opportunities, 38

J

Joint ventures, 75-77

K

L

Labor law, 80
Leverage Buy Out (LBO) 126-129
Lease breaking costs, 115
Legal records, investigation of, 71-72
Leverage ratio, 90
LIFO, 100, 31, G
Line of credit, G
Liquidation, 12, 98-99, 100, 114-122, G
Liquidation advantages, 121-122
Litigation, 32
Long-range plan, 24, 41, 54

M

Maastricht Treaty, 76
Market analysis, 23-24
Market segmentation, 23
Market value, 29
Marketing strategy, 23-24, 72
Merger, 5-8, 47 G
Mothball operation, 98

N

Negotiation process, 68-69
Net present value, NPV, 89, G
Net worth, 57, 98, G
Non-recurring costs, 99, 115
Notification, filing of, 16, 44-45, 48-49

O

Overseas acquisition, 76-78

P

Pac Man defense, 49, G
Pennsylvania corporate laws, 45-46
Poisin Pill, G
Pooling of interest, 29-30, G
Portfolio, G
Present value method, 58-59, 89, G
Price earning ratio (multiple), 58, 60, G

Pricing, method, 57-58
Pricing, strategy, 24
Prime rate, G
Pro Forma, G
Proxy, G
Purchase method, 29-30, G

Q

R

Redeployment of assets, 8101
Reinvestment, 95, 101, G
Reorganization,» G
Repatriation, 76, 78, G
Retained earnings, G
Retention analysis, 96-97
Return on Assets, ROA, 25, 40-41, 89-90, G
Return on Investment, ROI, 8, 10, 25, 40-41, 78, 101, G
Return on Sales, ROS, 40, 90
Robinson Patman Act, 72

S

Sarbanes-Oxley Act, 32, G
Sale of stock, 98, 105, 108-109, 112
Salvage value, G
Securities Exchange Commission, SEC, 16-18, 28, 44-49, 69, 80
    SEC Act 1933, 16-18, 44, 48
    SEC Act 1934, 16-18, 48-49
    SEC, registration requirements, 16, 48
Separation costs, 114
Shark Repellant, G
Sherman Act, 72
Sinking fund, G
Spin –off, 7, 106, 134, G
Split-off, 134, G
Split-up, 106, 134, G
Statutory laws, 18, 44-47, 76-77
Statutory mergers, 8, 12
Stock, G
Stock acquisition, 49
Stockholders, G
Stock market value, 57
Subchapter S corporation, 28
Systematic/unsystematic risk, 24-25

T

Take-over acquisition, 7, 47-48, G
Tax considerations, 9, 12-14, 100, 104-106
Tax free acquisition, 9, 12-14
Taxable acquisition, 12-14
Tender-offer, 12, 35, G
Traditional acquisition, 7
Treasury stock, 18
Treaty Establishing the European Community, 77
Treaty of Rome, 77
Trustee, G

U

Underwriter, G
Uniform Securities Act, 46

V

Vertical corporate growth, 5-6, 56
Vertical integration, 5-6, G

W

Warrant, G
Weighted average cost of capital (WACC), 134
White Knight, G
Working capital, G

Made in the USA
Lexington, KY
10 January 2013